SHOULD I GO TO MEDICAL SCHOOL?
An Irreverent Guide to the Pros and Cons of a Career in Medicine

Ali Binazir, M.D., M.Phil., Editor

SHOULD I GO TO MEDICAL SCHOOL?

ISBN 978-0-9779845-9-6

Should I Go to Medical School?: An Irreverent Guide to the Pros and Cons of a Career in Medicine. Copyright © 2017 Ali Binazir and American Council on Medical Education. All rights reserved. Except as permitted under the United States Copyright Act of 1976, no part of this publication may be reproduced or distributed in any form or by any means, or stored in a database or retrieval system, without the prior written permission of the publisher. It is illegal to copy, distribute or create derivative works of this book in part or in whole, or to contribute to the distribution, copying or creation of derivative works of this book. For information, address Elite Communications, 1618 Sullivan Ave #346, Daly City CA 94015.

This publication is designed to provide accurate and authoritative information regarding the subject matter covered. It is sold with the understanding that the publisher is not engaged in rendering professional services. If legal, accounting, medical, psychological, or any other expert assistance is required, the services of a competent professional person should be sought. The author and publisher specifically disclaim any and all liability arising directly or indirectly from the use or application of any information contained in this publication.
-- *From a Declaration of Principles jointly adopted by a Committee of the American Bar Association and a Committee of Publishers*

SHOULD I GO TO MEDICAL SCHOOL?

Table of Contents

1. SHOULD YOU OR SHOULDN'T YOU? 6
   Introduction: Why this book exists 7
   Why you should not go to medical school: a gleefully biased rant 11
   The two *real* reasons I didn't practice 23

2. THE VOICE OF REASON 27
   What it takes: first, evaluate your life 28
   The Aussie rural doc 30
   Emotional maturity, the secret sauce 31
   How to make better decisions about your future 33
   Integrating a medical career into a shared life 35
   The optimistic realist 37
   A view from the trenches: the MS1 39
   The wisdom of the unconventional primary care doc 43
   Rufus leaves medicine after 14 years 46
   Clinical medicine is service industry work 48
   Introverts, beware (and consider part time work) 49

3. AGAINST MEDICAL SCHOOL 51
   Premeds who reconsidered 52
   Against Medical School: The Med Students 55
      Before and After: How leaving medicine turned out for Jay . 56
      Jenny's having doubts 61
      How much debt again? 62
      Give me my money back 63
      Drops out after first year, switches to NP program 64
      To hell and back 65
      The future housewife with an MD 70
      Even the preclinical years? 72
      How Gavin got his groove back 73
      A medical student on leave 75
      Funny, but also really not funny 78
      The emotional burden of doctorhood 80
      The regret of the MS4 82
   Against Medical School: The Practitioners 83

I am not a discount shoe store 84
The clear-eyed orthopedist 85
The internist's mixed bag 86
The dangers of idealization 88
This is how you lose yourself 89
The suicide rate 92
Getting out before it was too late 93
The trauma of trauma surgery 95
Chief Resident looking for an off-ramp 97
The disillusioned neurosurgeon 98
Is the medical profession sustainable? 99
The MD/PhD's view 101
The whole story from the UK medic 103
Ideals, passion and hard work vs. reality of practice 106
The 20-year veteran with a heart of stone 108
The economics of Australian primary care 109
Medical profession's fine, but the medical professionals 110
The insecurity of the orthopedist 112
The fourth year resident who said sayonara 114
OB/GYN wants out 115
The well-tempered practitioner 116

4. FOR MEDICAL SCHOOL: Medical Students and Practicing Physicians Share Their Thoughts 118
For Medical School: The Med Students 119
Julie the MS2 120
Luigi the MS4, point-by-point 122
Nontraditional MS4 DO student 126
MS3 and loving it 128
What's your opportunity cost? 131
It's all about the right fit 132
For Medical School: The Practitioners 135
The minuses *and* the pluses 136
The radiologist living large 137
The ex-nurse 138
The secret trapdoor to debt-free med school 140
The small-town family practitioner 141
The neurosurgery resident 142

The mommy surgeon.. 143
The soldiering general surgeon 145
Good enough for this MD/PhD.................................. 147
It's a marathon, not a sprint 149
The view from sunny Portugal................................... 150
Christa, the resident who makes a difference 153

5. ON LIFESTYLE & RELATIONSHIPS 164

6. THE 360° VIEW FROM PRACTITIONERS 171
Interview with Dean Ornish, M.D. 172
Interview with Ashvin Pande, M.D., Interventional Radiologist 185

7. ALTERNATIVE CAREER PATHS 192
Why You Should Become a Nurse or Physician's Assistant Instead of a Doctor: The Underrated Perils of Medical School, by Jake Seliger... 193
Ryan the Naturopath.. 217
Physical therapy and pharmacology 219
A little time for microbiology 225
Research career 226
Final thoughts 237

8. ADDITIONAL RESOURCES 239

1. SHOULD YOU OR SHOULDN'T YOU?

SHOULD I GO TO MEDICAL SCHOOL?

Introduction: Why this book exists

The point of this book is to help you make a major life decision: should you pursue a career in medicine? This is a big-ticket item. Why? Because medicine isn't just a job, or even a career. It's a *calling*. Also, because this decision will determine the direction of *the rest of your life*. Hey, no pressure.

What the hell does a calling mean? It means that there are any number of jobs out there you could be qualified to do after 1-3 years of training. Web designer. Carpenter. Programmer. Banker. Hell, even lawyers start work after 3 years. But becoming a full-fledged doc takes around 12 years in the United States: 4 years of undergrad pre-med classes, 4 years of medical school, and 4 years of postgraduate training (internship and residency). It's the kind of profession that becomes not just a job but *your whole identity*. What other job changes the way people address you such that it supersedes *even your gender*? No longer Mr or Ms, but Dr, as in "Dr Jones to the ER, stat." Whether it's a guy doctor or a lady doctor is irrelevant — it's just *the doctor*.

So if you're going to invest that kind of time, energy (and money!) preparing for a career, it had *better* be a calling. Otherwise you're going to be miserable.

There. I've given away the punchline of the whole book, so now you don't have to read it anymore. But you already knew that. And you've probably already gone through my blog, and all the links attached to it, and most of the comments. I happen to know that you pre-med types are pretty thorough.

SHOULD I GO TO MEDICAL SCHOOL?

And if you have read all of those things, you will already know that my bias is towards discouraging most people from entering a career in medicine — *most*, but not all. To find out whether you are part of the "most" who'd be happier doing something else, or are one of the few that the world really needs to become a doctor, you may to have to read through this whole damn book.

That said, the purpose of this book is not necessarily to render a decision for anyone considering a medical career, but to help you *make an informed decision*. In the end you have to make the decision for yourself.

Wisdom comes from two sources: personal experience, or the borrowed experience of others. This book is mostly about the latter. Since you haven't gone through a medical career yet, you have no idea what you're getting yourself into. To say you know what being a doc is from watching one is like saying you know what it's like to get married and be a parent from watching your mom & dad. It doesn't work that way.

This is where other people's stories start to come in handy. You'll hear from the med students and residents; the disillusioned orthopedist of 14 years; the guy who goes to med school after 10 years in the military; the chief resident who quits in his final year; the 58-year old cardiologist with heartache; the blissfully content rural doc; the 35-year old obstetrician/gynecologist who suddenly feels stuck and can't escape; and dozens more, from both the pro and con contingents. This way, you get a flavor for what a medical career is like in each phase of training and practice.

By the way, if you were looking for one giant anti-med school screed, this ain't it. Hundreds of people have contributed stories of their experiences to the blog over the years, and all of their experiences are valid. So I have structured the book to give space to both the proponents of a medical career as well as the hell-no-don't-go camp. If you're looking for fodder for either argument, you will find it here.

The book has eight sections. The first, "Should you or shouldn't you," is the introduction and my essays.

Section 2, "The Voice of Reason," features balanced, well-reasoned pieces on what it means to be a doctor, with both the pluses and minuses. All but one of these come from practicing physicians.

Section 3 features pieces from medical students, residents and practicing physicians who warn *against* a medical career. Section 4 is from the proponents of a medical career.

Section 5 contains a few essays about lifestyle and relationships in the context of a medical career.

Section 6 features long-form interviews with two practicing physicians. One interview is with Dr Dean Ornish, a well-known figure in medicine and an eloquent proponent of it if there ever was one. The other is with Dr Ashvin Pande, interventional cardiologist and an old friend of mine.

Section 7 is about alternatives to medicine: naturopathy, physical therapy, pharmacy, physician's assistant, research, nurse practitioner, osteopathy, veterinary school, biomedical engineering.

The final section contains further resources: links to other books, videos and articles you may find useful.

SHOULD I GO TO MEDICAL SCHOOL?

The essays in this book come from all over the world: England, Australia, Portugal, America. Each has its own voice, which I have tried to preserve while editing them for readability. Most of the time, I translate the medical jargon, but sometimes I leave it in unexplained, because you're smart and curious and can totally figure it out and Google.

As you read the essays, remember that most of them started life as a comment on my blog. So when it says stuff like "If you are reading this article...", they are referring to my original blog post that got all of this started, which you are about to read next. And in case you were wondering, the *Ed* who leaves semi-snarky comments at the end of some pieces is the editor, yours truly.

SHOULD I GO TO MEDICAL SCHOOL?

Why you should not go to medical school: a gleefully biased rant

In the few years since I've graduated from medical school, there has been enough time to go back to medical practice in some form, but I haven't and don't intend to, so quit yer askin' already. But of course, people keep on asking. Their comments range from the curious — *"Why don't you practice?"* — to the idealistic — *"But medicine is such a wonderful profession!"* — to the almost hostile — *"Don't you like helping people, you heartless ogre you?"*

Since it's certain that folks will continue to pose me this question for the rest of my natural existence, I figured that instead of launching into my 15-minute polemic on the State of Medicine each time and interrupting the flow of my Hefeweizen on a fine Friday eve, I could just write it up and send 'em to the article. So that's what I did.

Now, unfettered by my prior obligations as an unbiased pre-med advisor, here are the myriad reasons why you should not enter the medical profession and the one (count 'em -- *one*) reason you should. I have assiduously gone through these arguments and expunged any hint of evenhandedness, saving time for all of you who are hunting for balance. And here are the reasons:

1) You will lose all the friends you had before medicine.

You think I'm kidding here. No, I'm not: I mean it in the most literal sense possible. I had a friend in UCLA Med School who lived 12min away, and I saw twice in 4 years. That's half a time a year. I saw her more often when she lived in Boston and I was in LA, no foolin'.

SHOULD I GO TO MEDICAL SCHOOL?

Here's the deal: you'll be so caught up with taking classes, studying for exams, doing ward rotations, taking care of too many patients as a resident, trying to squeeze in a meal or an extra hour of sleep, that your entire life pre-medicine will be relegated to some nether, dust-gathering corner of your mind. Docs and med students don't make it to their college reunions because who can take a whole *weekend* off? Unthinkable.

And so those old friends will simply drift away because of said temporal and physical restrictions, to be replaced by your medical compadres, whom you have no choice but to see every day. Which brings us to...

2) You will have difficulty sustaining a relationship and will probably break up with or divorce your current significant other during training.

For the same reasons enumerated above, you just won't have time for quality time, kid. Any time you *do* have will be spent catching up on that microbiology lecture, cramming for the Boards, getting some sleep after overnight call and just doing the basic housekeeping of keeping a *Homo medicus* upright and functioning.

When it's a choice between having a meal or getting some sleep after being up for 36 hrs vs. spending quality time with your sig-o, which one wins, buddy? I know he/she's great and all, but a relationship is a luxury that your pared-down, elemental, bottom-of-the-Maslow-pyramid existence won't be able to afford.

Unless you've found some total saint who's willing to care for your burned-out carapace every day for 6-8 years without complaint or expectation of immediate reward (and yes, these people do exist, and yes, they will feel massively entitled after the 8 years because of the enormous sacrifice they've put in, etc etc).

3) You will spend the best years of your life as a sleep-deprived, underpaid slave.

I will state here without proof that the years between 22 and 35, being a time of good health, taut skin, generally idealistic worldview, firm buttocks, trim physique, ability to legally acquire intoxicating substances, having the income to acquire such substances, high liver capacity for processing said substances, and optimal sexual function, are the Best Years of Your Life.

And if you enter the medical profession during this golden interval, you will run around like a headless chicken trying to appease various superiors in the guise of professor, intern, resident, chief resident, attending, and department head, depending on your phase of devolution -- all the while skipping sleep every fourth day or so and getting paid about minimum wage ($35k-$45k/yr for 80-100 hrs/wk of work) or paying through the nose (med school costing about $40-80k/yr). Granted, any job these days involves hierarchy and superiors, but none of them keep you in such penury for so long. Speaking of penury...

4) You will get yourself a job of dubious remuneration.

For the amount of training you put in and the amount of blood, sweat and tears medicine extracts from you (and I'm *not* being metaphorical here), you should be getting paid an absurd amount of money as soon as you finish residency. And by "absurd", I mean at least a third of what a soulless investment banker makes, who saves no lives, produces nothing of social worth, and is basically a federally-subsidized gambler (but that's a whole different rant, ahem).

I mean, you're in your mid-thirties. You put in 4 years of med school, and at least 4 years of residency (up to 8 if you're a surgeon). You even did a fellowship and got paid a pittance while doing that. And for all the good you're doing humanity – you are *healing people*, for chrissakes – you should get paid more than some hedge fund spreadsheet jockey shifting around numbers, some lawyer defending tobacco companies or some consultant maximizing a client's shareholder value, whatever the hell *that* means.

Right? *Wrong*. For the same time spent out of college, your I-banking, lawyering and consulting buddies are making *2-5 times* as much as you are. At my tenth college reunion, friends who had gone into finance were near retirement and talking about their 10-acre parcel in Aspen, while 80% of my doctor classmates were still in residency, with an average debt of $100,000 and a salary of $40,000.

5) You will have a job of exceptionally high liability exposure.

But wait, it gets better. Who amongst these professionals has to insure himself against the potential wrath of his own clients? The investment banker's not playing with his own money. And even if he screws up to the tune of, oh, hundreds of billions of dollars, nearly wrecking the world economy, Uncle Sam's there to bail him out (see: 2008-2009).

The lawyers? They're *doing* the suing, not being sued. But the doctors? Ah. Average annual liability premiums these days are around $30,000. That goes up to $80,000 for an obstetrician-gynecologist (who remains liable for any baby he/she delivers

SHOULD I GO TO MEDICAL SCHOOL?

until said infant turns 18) and into the six-digit realm for neurosurgeons. Atul Gawande wrote a dynamite article about docs' compensation in the 4 May 2005 issue of *The New Yorker* entitled "Piecework" — check it out.

6) You will endanger your health and long-term well-being.

The medical profession is bad for you. Just ask any current doctor or med student. You will eat irregularly, eat poorly when you do get the irregular meal (and sayonara to the now-outlawed drug-company sponsored meals -- god bless their bottomless pockets), have way too much cortisol circulating in your system from all the stress you experience, have a compromised immune system because of all the cortisol in your blood, get sick more often because of the compromised immune system (and the perpetual exposure to disease -- *it's a hospital where everybody's sick*, duh), and be perennially sleep-deprived.

If your residency is four years long, on average you will spend *one entire year of those four* without any sleep. *A whole year of no sleep.* Do you get that? This is as stupendously bad for you as it is for patients — you've heard of Libby's Law, right? Groggy doctors can kill patients when they don't mean to.

Groggy docs can also hurt themselves. One friend stuck herself with a needle as she was drawing blood from an HIV patient. She's fine now, but that was a good 9 months of panic (PS: she has since quit clinical medicine).

My good friend and college classmate James — a serious contender for the title of Nicest Guy on Earth — had a severe car accident one morning on the way to the hospital because he fell asleep behind the wheel. Luckily, his airbag deployed and he didn't suffer long-term injuries. Everyone seems to know already that medical care can kill patients (haven't read *The House of God* by Samuel Shem yet? Go get it now — brilliant and the second funniest book I've ever read, after *Catch-22*), but it's usually news that it can kill the docs, too.

7) You will not have time to care for patients as well as you want to.

This is how the math works: Many patients, few of you. Just one, actually, unless your name is United States of Tara (and no, multiple-personality disorder ain't the same as schizophrenia — I learned *something* from med school). So you have to take care of many patients. And if they're in the hospital, that means they're really sick, otherwise they'd still be at home.

So you are scurrying around trying to take care of all of them at once, which means that each individual patient can only get a little bit of your time. Which means that you won't have a chance to sit at the bedside of that sweet old vet and hear his stories of Iwo Jima. Or get to the bottom of why that LOL (*little old lady* — medical slang's been around way longer than internet slang, buddy, so laugh a little less loud) can't get her daughter to come visit. Or to do any of that idealistic stuff that you cooked up in your adolescent brain about *really connecting* with patients.

Get a grip! This is about action, taking care of business, getting shit done, making that note look sharp because the attending is coming to round in an hour and he's a hardass, and that's the difference between getting recommended for honors or just passing, so get on it already and quit yakking with the gomer. Which is an older patient with so many problems you should have never let 'em get admitted in the first place, acronym for *get out of my ER*, and I didn't make it up, so direct your righteously indignant wrath elsewhere, thank you very much). It's about CYA — *cover your ass*. For better or for worse, you just start to treat patients as problems and illness-bearing entities for the sake of mental efficiency ("55yo WM s/p rad prostatectomy c hx CHF & COPD"), which does not do much for your empathetic abilities. Which brings us to...

8) You will start to dislike patients — and by extension, people in general.

Okay, so now you're overworked, underpaid, underfed, and sleep-deprived. Whose fault is that? Well, it's not really the hospital's fault — it's just drawn that way. And it's not your boss's fault, because somebody has to take care of patients, and he can't do it because he's the boss, duh.

So whom to blame? Ah yes — patients. It's the *patients'* fault! They're the ones creating all the work! The ones who get in the way of your nap, your catching your favorite TV show, having an uninterrupted meal, getting together with your sig-o for some therapeutic nookie. How dare the gomer in 345E have an MI while you're watching *CSI*? Does she have any consideration, letting her blood pressure tank to 40 over palp at 3.30am, while you're making out with a supermodel on the shores of Bora Bora (assuming you're lucky enough to be actually asleep)?

The logic may be twisted — patients, on the whole, don't get sick deliberately just to spite you — but it is deeply ingrained in medical culture. Heck, there's even a slang term for it: a *hit*. As in, "We got four hits on our admitting shift at the ER today." Hit — the same way you would be struck by a mortar, bullet, shell, or bomb. Getting hit is a Bad Thing.

Patients aren't people, you see — they are potentially lethal disasters that can explode all over the place and ruin your whole day. *"We got hit again"* — one more patient to take care of, says the resident.

But really, is that resident blameless? Or how about Dr Hardass the attending and his intransigent ways? Hell, they're at fault, too!

Soon the circle of blame expands to the outer reaches of the cosmos, and every potentially accountable organism from amoeba to blue whale will be personally responsible for your misery. But lest you think we've forgotten you, remember — it's all still your fault, patients.

9) People who do not even know you will start to dislike you.

Once upon a day, in a time somewhere between the Cretaceous and Triassic eras, physicians were held in awe and respect by the general public. Their seeming omniscience was revered, and TV shows like *Marcus Welby MD* glorified their empathetic sangfroid and high-minded grace. Heck, they were even considered sexy or something.

I only noticed in recent years that this ain't the case no more, and doctors rank on the contempt scale somewhere above meter maids and at or below divorce lawyers (but still much higher than I-bankers and other invertebrates). The average Joe and Janet are tired of the ever-rising cost of medical care, tired of all the stories of malpractice, tired of the perceived greed of the pharmaceutical firms, tired of the heartless profit-focussed practices of insurance companies.

But where do they pin their frustration? To whom can they direct their ire? Insurance and drug companies are nameless, faceless entities, as are hospitals. We need a *person* to blame, like a nurse or a doc.

Nurses are overworked and massively underpaid, so it doesn't really make sense to get mad at them. But doctors — those darn Mercedes-driving, Armani-wearing, private-school using, golf-playing social climbers! By being the most visible symbol of the medical profession, the doctor will have the dubious distinction of being the scapegoat for all its maladies. Fair? Hell no — we already told you docs are overworked, underpaid, and often railing at the same injustices Joe and Janet are. Some of them don't even play golf! (They don't have time. Except for dermatologists and radiologists.) But such it is. Hey, I'm just letting you know which direction the rotten tomatoes are flying so you can consciously choose the "toss" or "splat" end of the trajectory.

10) You're not helping people nearly as much as you think.

So by now I may have managed to inspire your righteous indignation with some of the things I've said about the medical profession. But maybe in the back of your head, you were still thinking, "Well, even though it sounds like a bunch of bitter black bile, he does kinda sorta have a point." But even so, this here #10 will make any hominid with a heart blow his head off: *"Whaddya mean you're not helping people? Isn't that what medicine is all about?!?"*

SHOULD I GO TO MEDICAL SCHOOL?

Well, actually, yes and no. Sure, there is the immediate gratification of delivering a baby, fixing someone's eyesight with LASIK, catching a melanoma before it causes trouble, or prescribing some thermonuclear antibiotics to kick a nasty bronchitis before it becomes lethal pneumonia.

But, depending on the field you choose, most of the time you're not doing that. You're treating chronic conditions that are self-inflicted: emphysema, obesity, cardiovascular disease, diabetes. Moreover, patients tend to be non-compliant: they basically don't do what you tell 'em to do. In fact, *you too* are probably one of those non-compliant patients who doesn't exercise more, eat healthier, and take pills as they're prescribed. Anecdotally, 50%+ of prescribed medications are taken incorrectly or never.

So there you are, like Cuchulain the legendary Celtic warrior, wading into the ocean and, in your rage, trying to [fight the invulnerable tide](#) and improve the health of your patients. You pour all your earnestness, good intentions and expertise into it, and… not a whole lot happens. Your efforts bear no fruit. So you suck it down and move on, sustained by the occasional kid who does get better, that eyesight that does improve, that bronchitis that doesn't turn into pneumonia. Win some, lose many more.

AND THE ONE AND ONLY REASON WHY YOU SHOULD GO INTO MEDICINE:

You have only ever envisioned yourself as a doctor and can only derive professional fulfillment in life by taking care of sick people.*

There's really no other reason, and lord knows the world needs docs. Prestige, money, job security, making mom

SHOULD I GO TO MEDICAL SCHOOL?

happy, proving something, can't think of anything else to do, better than being a lawyer, etc are all incredibly bad reasons for becoming a doc.

You should become a doc because you always wanted to work for *Médecins Sans Frontières* and your life will be half-lived without that. You should become a doc because you want to be the psychiatrist who makes a breakthrough in schizophrenia treatment. You should become a doc because you love making sick kids feel better and being the one to reassure the parents that it's all going to be OK, and nothing else in the world measures up to that.

Or as my general surgery resident put it, you should become a doc because "my dad was an ass surgeon, my big brother's an ass surgeon, and by god I'm going to become an ass surgeon."

But woe betide you if there's anything else, anything at all, that would also give you that fulfillment. Because pursuit of medicine would preclude chasing down that other dream and a whole lot more — a dream that could be much bigger, much more spectacular, much more enriching for yourself and humanity than being a physician.

Just ask some of the guys who started out on the medical path but then veered off: John Keats, Walker Percy, Sir Arthur Conan Doyle, Giorgio Armani, or Michael Crichton. Actually, only Armani is still alive, so you can't really ask the other ones. And he's kinda busy anyway. But you can sort of ask the people in this book, who have provided candid viewpoints about how a career in medicine has turned out for them.

But before, we go to that, I have a little confession to make.

SHOULD I GO TO MEDICAL SCHOOL?

*Also acceptable: You want to get into academic medicine. Pretty much need an MD or MD/PhD as prerequisite.

SHOULD I GO TO MEDICAL SCHOOL?

The two *real* reasons I didn't enter the medical profession

So you just read about the 10 reasons why *you* shouldn't go to medical school. They're all very good reasons, but not necessarily *my* reasons why I didn't practice medicine. Heck, if it was just those, I'd probably put up with it. There were two main reasons why I chose to forgo the practice of medicine, and here they are, now in public for the first time:

1. I felt I was becoming less myself.

Recently, I read a fascinating article about a doc who had a rare neurological condition called mirror-touch synesthesia. This made him hyper-empathetic to the point of feeling the pain of his patients. *All of it.*

What struck me most about the article was that Dr Joel Salinas thought this was totally normal. Huh? Here's a guy with neurology that's almost superhuman, and he just assumes that the rest of the world must be just like him.

That's when I realized, oh crap — I've been doing the same thing my entire life! I don't quite have mirror-touch synesthesia, but apparently I'm wired to be much more empathetic than average. As a kid, I cried very easily. To this day, I can't watch scary or violent movies. And as a grown man, I still tear up pretty easily. And I assumed everyone else was just like that.

So in order not to be overwhelmed by the emotion and pain that I encountered every day in the hospital, I would shut down that whole empathy thing. That turned me into someone who wasn't me, which was not sustainable. Now I write self-help books, write poetry, help people get happier, read a few books a week, and teach topics that interest me. For me, this is much more sustainable.

2. Medicine was boring.

Waitasec. Let me get that straight. Did you say medicine was boring? Different patients every day, infinite variety, this vast body of knowledge? How can anyone get bored?

Well, I learn faster than the average person, and require a lot of novel stimulus to keep my brain interested. I read 100+ books a year. Which means that repetition bores me. Fast. And repetition is the very essence of medical practice. You do the same history and physical exam, same surgery, same spinal tap, same procedure, over and over again.

That is, unless you *specialize*. In which case things become even *more* repetitive. Generalists such as internists or family practice docs see a lot of different things in a given day. But when you specialize, you do just a few things over and over again. The upside is that you can then achieve something resembling mastery and become the very god of appendectomies, nose jobs, or chest x-rays.

For some people, this kind of repetition is the very definition of heaven. For better or for worse, that's exactly what drives me up a wall, which may explain why I had to go a more entrepreneurial, creative route.

A disclaimer

SHOULD I GO TO MEDICAL SCHOOL?

I tell you these things not just so you can have a better understanding of yours truly the author, but to see if you can recognize yourself in these patterns. Are you the hyper-curious person of the peripatetic mind? Are you a super-empath? Do you have entrepreneurial instincts? Then chances are that medicine will be a tough fit for you.

I'm guessing that some of you who are reading this book have had a lifelong dream of being a doctor. Or maybe everyone in your family is a doctor. Or you just read Oliver Sacks, and thought, "Goddammit, that's who I want to be." Or maybe you're the wunderkind in some economically disadvantaged part of the world, and becoming a doc would be this incredible coup to bring glory and wealth to yourself and your family.

You should know that I'm not any of those people. It's safe to say that there have not been ten consecutive minutes in my life that I've wanted to be a doc. I love *science*. I wanted to do theoretical physics, but after realizing that was not in the cards, decided to go into biological research (neuroscience, specifically).

Academic medicine was the way forward for that, so I applied for the Medical Scientist Training Program (MSTP), a highly selective full-ride MD-PhD program. That's what many of my Harvard friends did. I got in, but chose not to do it. Keep all this in mind before you compare yourself to me or take anything I say as gospel.

You should also keep in mind that I've never practiced as a licensed physician. That's why it's important to read these stories and hear firsthand accounts from practicing docs. Many of them corroborate what I've already said. And the general trend has been of the profession becoming less lucrative, more regulated, less autonomous.

But some docs love their work. So read the stories and see what resonates with you. You will never be able to live the lives that these storytellers recount, but I'm hoping this book is the next best thing. I wish you wisdom in your decisions.

2. THE VOICE OF REASON: GUYS WHO GET IT

SHOULD I GO TO MEDICAL SCHOOL?

What it takes: first, evaluate your life

Doing what you love is not easy in the world we live, but pursuing that goal should not be simply shut off. Chances are, you are currently either a premed, a medical student, or a physician having a bad day if you are reading this book.

If you are a medical student and you are unhappy, you need to really take a break when you find one, think about what the problem is, and actively look around you for the advice you need to achieve your goal of personal joy. The doctors are around you, and they are only a breath away from providing you with the advice based on true experience.

If you are a physician and you are reading it in serious unhappiness, you need to analyze your current situation. Look at where your life was, think about what your state of mind was when you started your journey, and actively look at the options you have for improving your life style.

You may be agreeing with this article based on your own experience; however, you shouldn't fill your mind with only the negativity of the profession. Talk with other physicians in your field who you can seriously pour your thoughts to without thinking of your ego, and discuss what the profession offers in terms of happiness. If the joy is unattainable, and you know you will never attain it based on good reasoning, then you need to weigh your options, or suffer the reality.

Finally, for the premeds out there who are just unsure: You are about to embark on a costly journey on many levels. It will take a mental toll, a financial toll, a social toll, and a physical toll. Do not think that you can make yourself immune to the trainings of a profession that warrants all these issues. Talk about them with the doctors you shadow. Evaluate your life, and ask yourself if you can take the journey.

Don't go into it because you are "gifted" or "smart." Don't go into it for the money. Don't go into it because you have the stats. Don't go into it because everyone wants you to. Don't go into it because it will make you look good. Don't go into it because it gives you prestige. Don't go into it because you didn't think of anything else to do with your life.

Go into it because you need every aspect of it in order to be happy. Go into it because your life feeds on extreme mental challenge. Go into it because the feeling you get from studying the hell out of organic chemistry releases an extreme amount of endorphins. Go into it because you're okay with that physics class taking over your life, and the pain and stress that other people talk about does not exist with you because you love to learn. What they call pain, you call feeding your lifestyle the joy and happiness it craves. Go into it because the medical world fascinates you. Go into it because you have weighed your options well, and you know that medicine is the only thing that can satiate your hunger.

Ed: Great piece! Agree with very nearly everything the author says, except for one: "Go into it because your life feeds on extreme mental challenge." Medicine ain't exactly theoretical physics — it's mostly glorified plumbing. The extreme mental challenge arises when you still have to make good decisions with 99% of your neurons shut down from sleep deprivation.

SHOULD I GO TO MEDICAL SCHOOL?

The Aussie rural doc

I'm an Australian doctor married to a doctor with an eldest daughter a doctor who was not persuaded by us to do something else.

After raising and educating our 6 children while a perpetual renter in the big city (paid too little to save deposit and buy large enough house) we moved to a remote rural community and took sole charge of the health of the town, loads of farms surrounding and a little rural hospital all in the second poorest postcode area in our state. We only charge the fee set by the universal "insurer" Medicare Australia; no out-of-pocket expense to any patient.

Ali Binazir has highlighted a lot of the downside of medical working conditions in the first world with intelligence and wit. While society refuses to pay full fare for health care and expects other people to sacrifice wealth, health and relationships in ways only expected by kids of their parents, practitioners of medicine can justly echo his words. Make the lifestyle of the doctors humane and caring and there will be many more of them, they will make fewer mistakes and make few complaints.

While people vote for tax cuts for themselves, higher wages for themselves and refuse their governments the power to subsidise the health care of the poor and disadvantaged, then the moral fault lies with them.

SHOULD I GO TO MEDICAL SCHOOL?

Emotional maturity, the secret sauce

I have worked with and around doctors for over 15 years now and I was even married to one for over 12 years. There is *one* element that separates the doctors that seem to not be able to see the forest for the trees and the ones that can peer through and see the light and *not* be crushed by the stress that seems to come from all sides from their perspective. That singular element is emotional maturity – that emotional element born *only* from life experience and perspective.

Greater than 90% of the people that become doctors follow a very structured existence from childhood all the way to doctorhood. They go from elementary, junior/senior high school and on to college then immediately (or nearly so) into medical school without ever being an actual adult in this world. They are always living under some umbrella or safety net. While they may have had a job or two in a grocery store or working at Best Buy, they never had to make sure that all the bills were paid or their kids were fed (they *were* the kid).

Most premeds trying to get into medical school never bore the ultimate responsibility for even their own existence. How are they expected to be able to look that kind of responsibility directly in the eye for someone else? The ability to handle the kind of pressures that these doctors lament is only developed from life experience..and they actually possess the least of all the people in the room. Common sense is also a casualty of the all too common life course to becoming a physician so how are they going to be able to put it all into perspective?

There is one very small segment of physicians that seem to handle all that the profession throws at them and march on unscathed. They are the few that luckily squirm their way into

SHOULD I GO TO MEDICAL SCHOOL?

medical school (usually D.O. school because M.D. schools won't even look at them) *after* having gained some life experience and real work experience. They *didn't* major in biochemistry or some other equally useless degree pursuit (useless unless they're headed for a career in research in that area) and they held real jobs and dealt with the real consequences of life. They were accountants, firemen, teachers and they had already put in some serious time away from their families and friends in order to get their meagerly remunerated careers going. They had to go back to school and add or retake some sciences, etc. and try to raise their GPAs and achieve well enough on an MCAT to be considered, even if just barely. They are probably some of the finest physicians in their fields.

Ed: Martin raises a good point: most people who go to straight to medical school out of college haven't really had a chance to develop life coping skills, and therefore ill-equipped to handle the rigors of medical training.

SHOULD I GO TO MEDICAL SCHOOL?

How to make better decisions about your future

I am now retired and some 55 years out of medical school. So, my view of things may be somewhat dated but not unrelated to a variety of medical experiences.

But first, I'd like to say a word about Dr. Binazir's essay which I read not long after he first published it. At that time I had had some of the same ideas and was trying to see if others had like thoughts. His was the only thing I found then and since I have found nothing of like value. I say 'value' because I strongly believe it is the type of thinking that anyone going into medicine (especially for a M.D.) ought to do. This is a matter of doing what the world of business and law requires — *due diligence*. Before entering into a contract-like situation an individual or company should thoroughly investigate the people, companies, associations, reputations, nature of the business, etc with whom you will be associating! Such a serious and in-depth investigation is needed to be sure that what you first thought was a "good deal" is indeed a good deal for *you* — the one who will have to live with the deal. At the present time the "it's good to go to medical school" people have near-to-exclusive access to the podium.

Dr. Binazir's essay is his view and I generally agree with him. He is generous and is to be thanked for maintaining this page. I have some additional thoughts along this line and could elaborate. I'm not interested in discussing whether or not someone ought to go to medical school, the problems of getting into medical school, which classes to take to get in, etc. I am too dated for that!

However, I am convinced there is a dearth of information about the negative side (past, present, and future) of a life in

SHOULD I GO TO MEDICAL SCHOOL?

medicine which should be considered by an 18-year old person before committing to 4 years of pre-med, 4 years of medical school, and 4+ years of residency before really going to work. This may apply even to some who have close associations with family and friends in medicine. The more information you have, both pro and con, the better equipped to make decisions about what you *ought* or *want* to do. I suspect that most people entering medical school even today really do not have the foggiest idea of what life in medicine will be like.

SHOULD I GO TO MEDICAL SCHOOL?

Integrating a medical career into a shared life

As a 50-year-old physician it was great to read and brought many smiles to my face. There is very little in it that can be denied and yet being an MD can still be a wonderful life. I totally identified with the 'Lost Decade' feeling. The 1-night-in-3 call-induced haze that was my 20s still feels like an amazing loss to me and yet there were many rewards along the way. I can even still remember some of them! Sleep deprivation is a bitch when it comes to long-term memory consolidation. I write this at 0130h the night after being awake 26 hours straight and coming home to sleep from 9am-3pm before heading off to see my 14-year-old daughter's hockey playoff game, having missed my son's game due to the call the night before.

I have been lucky to have been married to an MD classmate for 20 years and have 4 wonderful children. Certainly, physician relationships can survive, in my med school class, 9 couples formed and married. 8 of the marriages are still intact 25 years on. In my office practice group there are 9 physicians, all still married to their original spouses. Pretty impressive and probably aberrant but shows that it can be done. Truly though it is hard. I spent a few hours with a classmate who went into anaesthesia last week who I have only seen 3 times in 20 years after being great friends in both undergrad and med school, even though he lives only 20 minutes away! Was a wonderful visit! Hopefully they will occur more frequently.

I have been lucky enough to work and teach all over the world and I still greatly enjoy patients and the interactions I have with them. I enjoy the practice of medicine and surgery. What I don't enjoy is the politics and intrigue of dealing with hospital administrators and others in positions of power. But such is life; it is not all roses. At the end of the day, it will have been a wonderful life. Yes, it could have been much different, perhaps better, but it could definitely have been much worse and spent in much less useful ways.

Prior to my night on call last night, I spent 3 hours tutoring a group of first year medical students. I will share your post with them. I am sure that they have considered the points you have made, and to their credit have decided to give medicine a try anyway. As far as my own children, they will make their own decisions as to whether they have the drive and desire to pursue a career in medicine. I will not be disappointed if they don't follow in their parents' footsteps but I know that they will have missed something special.

SHOULD I GO TO MEDICAL SCHOOL?

The optimistic realist

I work as a doctor, and I am *happy*. There have been times when I am not, and there are sides to my job I don't like. But in life, I am happy.

I could list you all the things I would change in my life if I had a magic wand, but I won't; I don't have a magic wand.

I like to concentrate on the things that make me happy and fulfilled. How work makes me feel. How I spend my time off (unfortunately sometimes it is just catching up on sleep).

One thing I would like to add to the "do medicine/don't" debate is the emotional toll what you will inevitably see and experience will take on you. Things that to the general public are terrifying, horrific and a once in a lifetime occurrences, happen everyday. You see them everyday. Eventually you become numb. Things that initially devastated you because of how sad they were stop making you shed a tear. That's the part of medicine I don't like. I don't like the fact that things that used to affect me don't. That I have become hardened to some of the atrocities that the game of life deals. I haven't met a doctor yet who hasn't been hardened to some extent to the sad things we see day in day out.

But I am a sucker for happy. I like seeing and treating kids. I like making them feel a bit better, laughing with them, sending them home from hospital well again. I couldn't work in adult medicine. Chronic illness is one of the Western world's biggest problems and it is only going to get worse. I like to deal with the cute fluffy side of things, the (mostly) smiley reassurance I am able to give. My respect goes to the physicians who work day in day out with people who have self-inflicted diseases, that have no chance of a cure, just a way of slowing down the internal ticking time bomb of the last breath. I couldn't do that.

If you are going into medicine, think long. Think hard. Don't go in it for the money. Don't go in it for the glamour (let's face it, half the workforce wear glorified pajamas all day). Do lots of work experience. And if early on you don't like it, don't stick it out for the sake of it — get out.

Remember the world does need doctors, even if sometimes we are subjected to lawsuits and abuse, so if you are just having a bad day, week, month, stick at it for another six. You might find wandering around in pajamas, comfortable financially, but not rich, yet satisfied, is right for you. Try (I am unsuccessful) to live by the motto "What goes on in the hospital, stays in the hospital." That way you get a balance between life and work. But it's true, being a doctor means the hospital is going to take up more of your life than is ideal. But what job is ideal? I don't think anyone knows the answer to that!

SHOULD I GO TO MEDICAL SCHOOL?

A view from the trenches: the MS1

I'm a first year medical student. I wanted to share an honest breakdown of my thoughts so far:

1) Money: I'm not even done with one year of medical school and I just crossed the $100K mark on my loans (had some from undergrad). By the time I'm done with medical school I'm looking at nearly $400K in student loan debt at an averaged 6% interest. I live very frugally, rent sectional housing (double wide trailer), grow my own fruits and vegetables, and work 15 hours a week at the school library.
Some of my fellow students are taking out way more money than me and they will be nearing the $500K mark, justifying it by the fact they will be "making tons of money" when they are doctors. Sad to see people who have come this far and have no idea what they are getting into. Go onto any student loan site and type in these numbers. See what you come up with. My total loan repayment will be the equivalent of buying a 4 bedroom house, 2 average cars, and an all expenses paid around the world vacation.

2) Time: I average 12 hour work days. Mind you I'm in my first year of school and I'm working hard to prepare for boards. The good thing is I mostly make my own schedule. If it's a nice day I'll take a few hours in the morning and go fly fishing or trail running. On a rainy day I'll take some time at night and play video games or watch a movie. Some days, like today, I will study for around 16 hours straight, sleep for 6 hours, and repeat for the next few days before my test. I probably spend more time studying than most of my class, but I'm a slow learner. I rank in the middle of my class. Most of the people above me work harder, are gifted with photographic memory, or have a post-graduate degree in a medically related subject.

3) Relationships: I have an amazing girlfriend that I have been dating for the past year. We are very happy together but I will say our relationship would be better if I wasn't in med school. She lives 3 hours away and we spend 1-2 weekends a month together. The distance has been difficult but she is very, very, understanding. It also helps that she is as busy as I am during the week with her job. We spend summers and vacations together and video-chat twice a day. I am not sure what the future holds for us but I am optimistic. She knows that I won't always be there, that my patients will come first, and sometimes I'll be exhausted, frustrated, or sad. Sounds cliché but she's different from most girls and I think we can make it work.

I haven't seen my "pre-med friends" in months, but I do my best to stay in touch with them. I have it easy here because I've lived all over the country and have experience staying in touch with people and making new friends.

Most of the people in my class are socially awkward. I have a small group of friends and we study together and hang out when there's time.

4) Happiness: Am I happy? Yes, because I choose to be. It's easy to surround yourself with people who complain and fall into that trap. I take my life one day at a time. I'm taking aim at my future, remembering my past, but focusing on the present.

5) Physical well-being: I'm not in terrible shape, but this is the worst shape I've been in my whole life. Medical school is very sedentary. I eat very healthy, try to exercise every day, but the effects of sitting down 10-12 hours a day take their toll. I've had a host of illnesses in the past year that are likely a result of stress and lack of sleep. I would say this is the #1 problem I have with med school. I need to find better ways to release stress because I know it only gets worse.

6) Outlook: I really am worried about what's going to happen to America's healthcare system. I think as a whole we are going in the wrong direction. However, I am very optimistic for my career as an individual because:
a) I know the career I've chosen is not for the faint of heart. I took several years off between undergrad and med school. I knew what I was getting into before I started. I know most doctors don't recommend it or wouldn't do it again. I don't care. I'm doing it because I can't see myself doing anything else and I love it.

b) I absolutely do not expect to "get rich" from medicine *at all*. I have a very realistic, some would even say pessimistic view on compensation. *Anyone who expects to get rich as a doctor is severely misguided and should not go into medicine! You will be miserable!* The fact is, doctor's salaries are going down and will continue to do so until the system breaks. I feel bad for physicians who rely on their practices as their sole means of income. I have a history as an entrepreneur: I've started and sold businesses in the past. I'm going into medicine with an entrepreneurial mindset and knowing that I will have to rely on a side-hustle to live a comfortable life.

c) I love medicine, I love people, and I love learning.

My advice: Take a year or two off before going to medical school. Know what you're getting into. Understand how

SHOULD I GO TO MEDICAL SCHOOL?

much money $500k is and how loans work. Please note that medicine is not "an easy way to make a few hundred thousand a year." Shadow as many doctors as you can and ask questions about their happiness, income, etc. Understand our country's current state. Learn about the Affordable Care Act!

And no matter what, *know that it's okay not to go to medical school.* It's not for everyone! You can live a life of service, importance and wealth without being a doctor. But to those of you who choose medicine: welcome, and good luck.

SHOULD I GO TO MEDICAL SCHOOL?

The wisdom of the unconventional primary care doc

I went into medicine a bit late, having worked as a musician for 17 years prior to starting medical school in my late 30s. Interestingly, I was not the elder statesman. There were 5 people older than me in my graduating class.

Medical school was a drain but a very rewarding experience. Relationships I made have continued to this day and I still carry fond memories of the rigors and challenges we faced individually and together. It doesn't bother me that many of the things I needed to learn aren't used in my day-to-day practice. While this could and should be examined and changed, I guess I was always able to keep my eye on the prize of seeing patients and building a career in medicine.

Residency, as well, was rewarding — more so, because we focused on the things we'd be doing in our careers. Sleep deprivation and pushing, pushing, pushing to get through the mountains of "to do's" were the norm, but it was also thrilling to dig down deep and do the best I could.

I chose primary care because it was the best fit for me and for my personality. I truly love seeing patients. Not *every* patient, to be sure, but I really look forward to building relationships and to being there in the way that a doctor should. We see people when they are most vulnerable, most frightened, most angry, most elated. We often share these experiences on a level which is deeper and more intimate that many family members would share with a patient.

SHOULD I GO TO MEDICAL SCHOOL?

But, medicine isn't for everyone, that is for sure. And, medicine won't help people find happiness. In fact, it will work against that goal. If you can do the personal work to find happiness within, then medicine can be very rewarding.

I often tell prospective physicians as well as colleagues who are struggling that they had better plan to spend as much time and energy finding life balance as they spent learning the Krebs cycle, renal physiology or keeping up with what meds are now on formulary. If doctors don't work to find a way to balance their career, family, relationships, hobbies, etc., then medicine will be very demanding and unrelenting, and finding satisfaction will be nearly impossible.

Finally, as to the worries about being unable to see the good you're doing or make a difference in a patient's life, (especially as it relates to chronic disease states in the self-harming patients described in numerous earlier posts), I would counter by saying that looking for this immediate confirmation of the worth of your interaction is the wrong goal. We shouldn't counsel patients about the dangers of hypertension with the expectation that they will do whatever we want and will agree with our recommendations without question. Furthermore, we shouldn't look for improved outcomes as an measurement of our effectiveness (although, we should always be hoping for good outcomes, of course.)

Rather, we should measure our success by the effort we put forth, because that is really the *only* thing we have any control over.

I remember one of my mentors in medical school, a pediatric gastroenterologist, asking me once how I would know if I had done a good job. I replied that I would make sure my patients liked me and that they all "did well."

His response was amazingly curt (and it remains some of the best advice I've ever received): "Don't fall into the trap of measuring you worth as a physican to a patient's opinion of you or whether or not they get better. Instead, ask yourself, 'Did I do the very best today that I could?' If you can answer, 'yes', then it has been a good day, *and that has to be enough.*"

Words to live by, not just in medicine.

Ed: As Krishna says in the Bhagavad Gita, you are entitled to your labors, but not the fruit of your labors. Thanks to Mark for sharing the story of his unconventional career path.

SHOULD I GO TO MEDICAL SCHOOL?

Rufus leaves medicine after 14 years

I left medicine after 14 years of practice and it is one of the best decisions I have ever made. Having spoken to many people, it is obvious that a huge variety of opinions on the matter exist and there is no broad consensus or feeling on how good or bad medicine is in general.

I have heard in person and seen on the internet the often strongly worded, and sometimes even bigoted things people write many would vigorously defend how good it is as a career. I have several hopefully well-balanced things I'd like to add. Mainly, I'd like to emphasise that choosing to study medicine is a huge and ultimately fairly unwise risk.

1. It is not for everyone; it is impossible to characterise any single type of person who likes medicine but often they are fanatics, quite happy to forgo a normal life for one reason or another. Many happy doctors are not normal people.

2. Some who say it is good genuinely love it, but many who say so are merely voicing a defence mechanism they use to cope with the difficult life decision of deciding to live with a career they secretly hate, i.e. they are lying to themselves and everybody else around them in order to manipulate themselves into facilitating the hard decision to stay in medicine over the arguably equally hard decision that leaving would entail.

3. The lives of so many doctors are so taken over by their work that they eventually lose sight of what a normal life is and how much better life could be outside medicine. They think they have it good.

SHOULD I GO TO MEDICAL SCHOOL?

4. The people prospective med students are at the age of 16-18 when they decide to commit to a medical career by their choice of subject matter *[in Commonwealth countries - Ed.]* are in many ways very different to the people they will become after finishing medical school at 24 and then again when finishing a residency and all the crap that comes with it at maybe 35. They are much less life-experienced, with different needs and mentality, and are in many ways different people. Many will not regret their decision, but many do and the rub is that it is impossible to know unless you have been there in a career level job.

For those who discover at this late stage in their lives that is was all a bad mistake, you have a stark and horrid choice: choose to be stuck in a career you hate for the next 25-30 years, yearning for retirement from age 35 onwards; or choose to accept that you have wasted vast amounts of money and the best years of your life to learn this hard lesson and to start at the bottom rung of something else at age 35. The bottom line is that however you look at it, choosing to study medicine is a massive risk and if you like it, jackpot, if you don't, square one again. Believe me, many doctors are stuck and counting the years. Ugh. Nobody tells you this and it is not as obvious as you think as many 18-year old wannabe doctors are idealistic, have an unwisely high ambition to realism ratio, and hear nothing except how good medicine is. You have been forewarned.

SHOULD I GO TO MEDICAL SCHOOL?

Clinical medicine is service industry work

No one ever tells you this explicitly, but seeing patients is all about customer service. Think being a waitress or retail store worker or cashier. One can be the most competent and thorough and diligent physician out there, thinking hard about your patients' problems in a medical and intellectual sense, but in the end, it's all about dealing with people.

When dealing with people from the general population you get the good, the bad, the ugly, and every subtlety in between, and people's attitude toward you really can be no different from what they expect from anyone else in the service industry — give them what they want, when they want it. And they wanted it *yesterday*. And you have to manage this all in an extremely short amount of time for each patient visit, all the while maintaining your actual clinical standards.

And when you consider that we are in an era of online ratings, which have infiltrated medicine, and when Press scores and patient reviews become metrics by which you will get paid, you really see how it's a customer service game. This is hardly how I would imagine those considering entering medicine think of the profession, or would want it to be. They think of the intellectual effort, the clinical mysteries, the fascinating diseases and pathophysiology — all that goes out the window pretty quickly when one's interesting clinical case has a seriously bad attitude or gives a really unclear history during the encounter, or wants medically inappropriate testing or care that you have to convince them is not necessary.

Introverts, beware (and consider part time work)

The challenge of dealing with the general population in a service sense is not only financial, but emotional and psychological, too. If you're introverted, like many science-leaning people are, you are going to contend with a very high risk of burnout and the so-called "compassion fatigue" on a daily basis.

Imagine seeing 20+ patients (a low average for a primary care doc), and you can see where this is going. It's rough. It's assembly-line style. And it's not for everyone, to say the least. This might be more an issue for people deciding which specialty to go into, but the fact is that most doctors are not pathologists or radiologists (those who don't see patients directly), so it seems to me most physicians are going to experience this customer service issue and need to be warned about it. I certainly wish I was.

The only way I manage to decompress as a strongly introverted primary care physician who sees ~24 patients a day is to work part time. I work 3 days a week. The off days make it possible to recharge, which is something all introverts need in order to stay sane. You make less than full-time work, but what you gain in sanity is precious.

If you are open to it, you can become more human

Medical school and a career in medicine, particularly clinical medicine, humanizes us in ways we can't imagine, and teaches us how to live and be empathetic — much in the way that people say that literature or fiction "teaches us how to live." When you encounter people from all walks of life and hear so many different experiences from people's lives, you can't help but become more in tune with moral complexity and the universality of the human experience, from suffering and pain to happiness and struggle.

This is meaningful, whether the crazy work day allows you to feel that on a given day or not. Whether it's fulfilling is another story. But it is meaningful. The more time you have to decompress between work days, the more you can appreciate this aspect of a career in medicine, and the more you allow yourself not to be hardened by everything that you experience that is unpleasant about it.

— Christine Casas, MD, FAAP

3. AGAINST MEDICAL SCHOOL

Premeds who reconsidered

SHOULD I GO TO MEDICAL SCHOOL?

A fourth-year college student weighs his options
I am a fourth year undergraduate, and for the first three years of my college career, I had made up my mind that I wanted to go into medicine and I did everything that I had to to get in. But in my last year, I began having some serious doubts as to whether committing another 4 years of my life, 3-7 years of residency, and being close to $200,000 in debt would be worth it in the end, not to mention the lifestyle I might have as a practicing physician.

What really hit me was when a few residents told me that if they could go back, they'd probably go into another profession. So now I'm freaking out, talking to different physicians, and am also looking into alternatives such as PA or Dentistry. The two options I'm weighing are: Would I regret going to PA or Dentistry feeling that I could have made it through MD school and that I underachieved/doubted myself or would I regret it more if I did go to MD school and it wasn't what I expected.

Ed: If this story sounds familiar to you, it's because a lot of premeds think this way. Just remember that medicine is a calling, not some prize to be won to gratify your ego. If you're having doubts this early in the process, it's probably the wrong profession for you.

I know I *can* do it — but should I?

I'm in the application process right now and have another interview in February but I don't think I'm even going to go. I have done very well in undergrad and worked an extremely hard job in Alaska with long hours and little sleep. So I know that I *can* become a doctor. But it wasn't until a few weeks ago I thought about if I *should* become a doctor.

I do like helping people but I don't think I'm passionate enough to go through medical school and put up with all the negative aspects. There are a lot of other careers that I can see myself going into and I know I will be successful. I guess I had been fighting to become a doctor to prove to myself that I could but that's not a good enough reason. Thanks for saving me years of my life and hundreds of thousands in debt.

Against Medical School: The Med Students

SHOULD I GO TO MEDICAL SCHOOL?

Before and After: How leaving medicine turned out for Jay

Before

Wow, you hit the nail on the head. I hated my first 2 years of med school, but told myself, "Everyone hates these 2 years. Just wait until 3rd and 4th year." Those years came and it was disappointment after disillusionment. I didn't know what the hell I wanted to do so I signed up for a prelim IM. I got 7 months into it and still didn't have a clue. I said to hell with it and started thinking about what I really wanted to do with my time and my life.

That being said, everything above is completely true. I can add some more as well. How about getting sick of self-inflicted diseases, ignored advice, back-talking alcoholics, drug-abusing pregnant mothers etc, all of who tell the doc to fuck off cause they'll do as they please? Or the way the fields have been relegated to cookbook and cookie-cutter practice in a lot of ways. Follow the guidelines or else, and never mind that the patient is an individual because it's in a study so it applies to all patients of this age group.

Being a physician, or a surgeon especially, is more akin to working both as an auto repair mechanic and a complaint desk simultaneously for 90 hrs/wk. Then there is the fun in discovering that the treatment you've been prescribing for the past several years because the studies said it was the correct thing to do — well, it's no longer correct because new studies say it's doing harm.

The script-farming drug seekers should be mentioned. They're fun to deal with (sarcasm). One of my personal pet peeves is when the 94 year-old patient, demented and barely alive due to a ton of other medical problems, comes in and the surgeon thinks a total colectomy is needed. Can't let the poor guy die in peace, we have to put him through surgery and let him die in recovery. Nice.

Malpractice was mentioned, but health insurance in general is a nightmare. In what other business does someone else tell you what you will accept as payment. The doc thinks the surgery is worth $300 due to time, overhead, etc, but insurance comes in and says "NO, you get $150 or nothing." That is why your face time with the doc is barely 10 minutes. If they don't rush though the patients they lose money for the day. Too many days of that and no more practice.

Then there's insurance directing patient care in the form of "you can't prescribe that until you've tried this for 5 months," or "you have to get an ultrasound before we'll pay for the CT." Nevermind the patient's co-morbidities [*concurrent diseases - Ed.*] or current ICU condition that make the insurance company's demands completely foolish, irrelevant and a waste of both time and money. You'll do it because they demand it. If insurance is bad enough as it is, I won't even get into the nightmare of red tape and dictated services that will be government-paid universal health care. I believe our litigious society was mentioned above.

I could go on and on, but this was your rant, not mine. I went to med school for all the wrong reasons anyway. First, both my parents are docs and one was pushing for it, but what's funny is that the other warned me and told me to run as far away as I could.

SHOULD I GO TO MEDICAL SCHOOL?

Second, I went for a biology degree because I put no thought into where I was going and by my third year I realized that it was either med school or work in a molecular bio lab (I hate lab work).

Third, I was naïve and believed I could work hard in school for a job that would allow me to put in less hours and still make very good money. Wrong. It sets you up to work longer hours under more stressful conditions. You don't get a break until you're the 65 y/o senior partner with residents and junior partners to do all the heavy lifting. Even still, I had a 64 y/o surgery attending putting in 96 hrs/wk and hating life because the bills (home and office) needed to be paid. No thanks.

Finally, I wanted to be part of a noble profession that helped people and made a difference, and I did to an extent. There are still the few patients I remember that I know I helped, but they were so few and far between it just didn't cut the mustard.

So now the field has one less doc, and I'll leave with this. A surprisingly high number of the physicians that I explain my situation to agree and are looking to retire early, wished they would have gotten out when I did, or better yet not have gone to med school in the first place.

After
I had a post above from a few years ago and thought it would be fun to post a follow up and some response to other posters. Looking back on that now my previous post reads harshly, but I still agree with most all of it. Most all docs I've worked with then and talked to since have said they wouldn't do it again or recommend it to their kids.

SHOULD I GO TO MEDICAL SCHOOL?

Despite that I do remember 3 or 4 who truly loved what they did. I suspect they knew this before entering medical school and did not apply for prestige, income, authority, respect, etc. So yes, those people are out there. However, the sacrifices all of them make are very real and reflected in the original article and my post above, albeit in a bitter tone. I'd suggest looking up alcohol/drug abuse, divorce and suicide rates among physicians compared to other professions simply to point out comparative stress levels. An OB/GYN relative of mine had two attempts herself.

As for myself since the post above, I've moved on to an ancillary health profession similar to posters above doing PT and Pharm. I have a 40hr week, a very nice paycheck, no malpractice, no insurance hassle, lots of time with the wife and kids, ability to relocate almost anywhere, in very high demand, and I still help people. I've set up a life for myself that I couldn't have begun to have in medicine, nor can my engineer brother or attorney sister-in-law.

For me it is a much improved lifestyle and I wouldn't go back for anything. I'm glad there are those few who truly enjoy it because it's certainly a noble and necessary profession. I just feel sad for those who are unhappy doing it but are stuck in it because of debt, mortgage, kids — as well as those who simply do it for their own ego. In older times it was respected. Today nobody cares that you're a doc except family members and other docs.

Clearly different people are fulfilled by different means and some will love medicine for its challenge, responsibility, and impact on patients lives. So for anyone reading this, maybe medicine is your place and you know you'll love it. However, even then the sacrifices are still very real, so do your research, shadow several docs and ask the hard uncomfortable questions before applying.

For anyone else applying because parents expect it (as was my case) or income, ego, status or whatever other reason I highly recommend against it and predict deep disappointment. There are other options that provide more personal time, money, status or whatever else it is you're looking for that don't put patient's lives at risk while you figure it out. That's one other reason I left. I knew that my discontented attitude was inherently leading to a disservice to my patients despite really wanting to do my best for them. My heart simply wasn't in it.

Good luck.

SHOULD I GO TO MEDICAL SCHOOL?

Jenny's having doubts

I appreciate this article and comments. I am currently a medical student and am starting to have serious doubts. I do not want to invest any more time and money into this profession and need to make a choice soon. I have been looking at the various specialties and just can't find one that seems worthwhile. I have an interest in Psychiatry, but am having doubts over this profession. I would appreciate any advice. Thank you.

SHOULD I GO TO MEDICAL SCHOOL?

How much debt again?

$100,000 in debt seems so quaint by today's standards. Barring the filthy rich, $175,000-$300,000 is becoming the norm, and the government just decided that residents don't deserve deferment on their 6-figure loans. So every year we're slaving away at minimum wage, we get to pay 4-5 figures in interest.

Ed: Median debt incurred from attending medical school hovers around $140,000-$160,000 as of 2016. This does not include college debt.

SHOULD I GO TO MEDICAL SCHOOL?

Give me my money back

I'm a 4th year medical student applying for residency positions. I definitely would not reapply to medical school knowing what I do now. My limited free time is spent searching for ways to pay off my loan debt without pursuing a residency and clinical practice. If someone were to give me $196,000 today, I would walk away and never look back.

SHOULD I GO TO MEDICAL SCHOOL?

Drops out after first year, switches to NP program

I dropped out of medical school 1 month ago for these exact same reasons! Finished my first year with an average GPA of 3.0 (B). I was doing well except of course for ALL the aforementioned reasons.

I think most people going into medicine are really quite naive. Social standards of "Oh shit he's a doctor" are much to greater than realistic life. It's not all its cut out to be. Now I'm $47,000 in debt but got out in time.

What am i doing now? I'm going for a career as a nurse practitioner. NP's are the future of medicine. Not much malpractice, insurance pays more percentage of procedures and about 100% the same scope of practice as a family medicine doc. Don't be fooled; find out what you're getting yourself into before you make this life-changing decision.

SHOULD I GO TO MEDICAL SCHOOL?

To hell and back

I decided that I wanted to become a doctor when I was three. I am twenty-two now. For 15 long years, all I did was toil for med school. I skipped prom, graduation, school dances, all those "fun things" people do in high school... just for medical school. And I got in. Yay for me.

Then med school started.

Mind you, I wanted to go into research. Still do. Medicine – as a scholarly endeavour – is fascinating. But unfortunately, people just don't see the truth until they're knee-deep in the mire called medical school, and by that time, you've invested too much of your life, money, energy, and your entire being to run away.

What was so depressing is this: I wasn't even helping people. In fact, most of the time people died anyway. I saw three patients die during one year, and what was even more terrifying, I stopped feeling anything. My grandmother passed away a few days ago, and while I had only met her when I was a toddler, my first reaction to being awoken and hearing the news was, "Aw dang it, couldn't you leave me alone?! I was going to sleep in."

People ceased to look like people; pain was just another symptom that needed to be examined. I could not be there when my boyfriend had a mental breakdown and attempted suicide; I was far too tired, far too worn out. Knowing that my cadaver had a son, a wife, and grandchildren, we mercilessly tore him apart without much feeling, shredded him into bits to the point that he was indistinguishable from the hunk of beef sitting in a fridge.

SHOULD I GO TO MEDICAL SCHOOL?

Teamwork? What teamwork? At my medical school people were so cutthroat they'd rip out pages of textbooks so others could not use them (and since our medical school gave you a list of "suggested textbooks" that was over 40 textbooks, no way was I buying them all). Attending physicians use nurses like toilet paper (from what I've seen), nurses treat interns like carpet and medical students are just pesky nuisances. Teamwork does not imply being with someone; it just implies you do the best you can do, or otherwise you'll have someone else *very* pissed at you for having to wipe after your mess. You think the assistant surgeon is there to help the main surgeon? No! The assistant is too busy minding his own job to care about anything else. Everybody's walking a tightrope.

So don't write about "being there" and all that twinkle-eyed hoopla, please. I was there for three years, and by the end of it, my hair (naturally raven) had turned auburn from just not sleeping or eating. My weight had yo-yoed between dramatically underweight and regular weight. My ulcer worsened, my migraine came in waves everyday, I became photosensitive and my depression worsened. I was on a cocktail of pills. Caffeine no longer worked and I was seriously considering Adderall.

My boyfriend (bless him for all his patience) could just watch me spiral down into a chaotic mess. Half my friends hated me (I either didn't have any time, or when they complained of any pain I just didn't feel for them), half my friends pitied me. I was broke (those books are expensive). I was stressed, and that showed – clearly – in my attitude. I kept getting sick. My menstrual cycle stopped. My brain felt as if it was full of unconnected factoids about medicine (which is an indictment to British medical education. Pressure *does not* move, and giving me a list of "what to do when diabetes hits you" won't

SHOULD I GO TO MEDICAL SCHOOL?

help me if I get a patient with an MI *and* diabetes). I read and read, and nothing seemed to make sense anymore. I guessed on my exams on histology and I aced it. I studied my rear end off for biochemistry and I barely passed. Nothing seemed to make any sense.

I am now an undergraduate at an American university, studying Physics. I am reapplying to medical school, not because I want to, but I have realised that I am not a full person unless I have those two letters after my name, a license to practise, and consigning myself to torture for the rest of my life (at least I am trying to do research, not practise!). I learn better, study better, in an orchestra; if I could change my path, I would, but I do not want to live the rest of my life seeing people in white coats and thinking "I could have been one of them".

Medicine is not a career that saves lives. It is a career in which you will see most people die (compared to any other career). I don't know anyone who said, "I care about my patients, each and every one of them." I have seen many say, "they're starting to look like bags of excrement and organs."

I hate people in general; how can I, when I took pains to explain *exactly* how to take the pills, then the patient comes back three days later, evidently not having listened to what I've said then screeching at me?! That happened to me in my third year, and it was the last straw. My health advisor told me, "Perhaps you shouldn't consider a career in medicine if you don't like people." Unfortunately he's a biologist, and he was never exposed to *The House of God* or *Mount Misery*-type of situation.

SHOULD I GO TO MEDICAL SCHOOL?

So here are my two cents: if you are dreamy-eyed and thinking of "helping people" and saving starving children in Africa and all that, then don't do this. You will probably see more children die than anyone else you know, and by the end of it you won't even feel anything. The people you are trying to help will hate you and will probably try to sue you for some nonsense. You'd be lucky to see your child once a day and your spouse will find someone who cares and leave (happened to my high school friend's parents).

If you are indeed like House [*the obsessive TV physician - Ed*], and can do *nothing* but practise medicine (I mean, he's a mess — no social life, no social skills, no personal life, no family, no happiness), then become a doctor. There is nothing else you can do. If you're in your twenties and spent more than half your life on this career path, you might as well as go with it and see it through because otherwise half your life would have meant nothing career-wise.

What of me? I am slowly recovering. I am still subject to hysterical outbursts, violent mood swings, insomnia. Thankfully my boyfriend seems happy being left alone (he's in a rigorous physics graduate program), and just as medicine is my first priority physics is his, so we suit each other well. My parents have been the most supportive; they scolded me, encouraged me, told me to live when I left med school (suicide attempt #3 and #4). I can laugh now, enjoy classes.

I remember on my white coat ceremony, the person who gave me the white coat and a pager jokingly told us that God gives all the doctors and doctors-to-be pagers and when the pagers break, we die. We all laughed then. I cannot laugh now.

SHOULD I GO TO MEDICAL SCHOOL?

Want an insight to what it's like to be in med school? A blog by a UCLA med school student said something similar to what a lot of people said here: medicine is not a career. It becomes your life. Do you want your job as your life?

SHOULD I GO TO MEDICAL SCHOOL?

The future housewife with an MD

I'm a second year medical student and this really hits home. How many times can you tell yourself that the next year will get better. First you have to just get past gross anatomy, then everything is down hill from there. Oh wait, then there is the Step 1 of the Boards (no pressure there, only going to determine the rest of your life), *then* it's all down hill.

Oh wait… third year is pretty terrible too. But at least you don't have to study all the time, right? Surely by 4th year its all down hill, besides stressing about interviews and matching and getting a good residency program. And then only 4-8 years of working your ass off, losing all your friends, relationships, and youth.

Since the first week of school I wondered if I was doing the right thing. Before starting med school, I focused so much on *getting in* that I never actually thought about what it was going to be like once I *was* in!! No matter how many people told me how miserable it was, I always made excuses…"Oh, it can't be *that bad*!!" IT IS.

I have already witnessed multiple relationships fail, including my own. Oh, that just means it wasn't meant to be, right? Hell no, that means that med school is ruining your life! I'm 24 years old and in the best shape and the best looking I'll probably ever be. But that doesn't matter because I don't have time to go anywhere or meet anyone so I might as well be fat and ugly for all it matters. And by the time I will have time to go anywhere and meet anyone, I probably will be fat and ugly.

SHOULD I GO TO MEDICAL SCHOOL?

Well I figure I might as well finish the 2.5 more years and get in as much debt as possible. Then I can do whatever I want. Nothing wrong with being a housewife with an MD, right?

SHOULD I GO TO MEDICAL SCHOOL?

Even the preclinical years?

I am in my second year of medical school (so I'm still only in the classroom) and I have already witnessed some of the disadvantages of medical school that you have listed. People have broken up with their significant other; some even got divorced. It is hard to see many of my friends. Some of my classmates are already sleep-deprived.

When Dr Binazir first wrote this article, he mentioned the average debt after graduation to be $100,000. According to AAMC, the median debt for 2014 is now $162,000. So the newer doctors are going to stay broke for a longer time than before. If you are considering applying to medical school, think about it real carefully. On the plus side, as a doctor, you'll pretty much always have a job.

SHOULD I GO TO MEDICAL SCHOOL?

How Gavin got his groove back

I went to medical school straight out of college, bringing with me a love of learning and a broad set of knowledge. I wanted to earn a MD/MPH and do something *big*.

What followed was years of depression, anxiety and anger. Instead of something BIG, I ran straight into the memorization olympics. Most of my classmates were professional memorizers (and expert whiners) who didn't really care about science or medicine. This was an expensive, private school and most everyone were there for the career – the high-paying specialties. It was hard to make friends.

After banging my head against the wall for three years, I quit the MD program. It's been six months and I'm slowly re-integrating with society, getting my strength back, becoming my old self again. I went back to my old passion (long since thrown away) and now study science journalism at a big, broad university. Crazy that I used to think med school was a place for science lovers.

Once a week, I stop by my old med school so I can complete the MPH. I should hate the place, but I feel good when I go back, because I remember how happy I was (early on) and how I dreamed of doing something great as a physician. I also know, without a doubt, that I never want that life again.

I don't regret going and I don't regret leaving. I just wish I had the courage to leave sooner. Harder at 22 than at 25, I suppose. Now I have the freedom to put my ambition someplace real.

SHOULD I GO TO MEDICAL SCHOOL?

Ed: I believe an MPH is one of the noblest degrees out there. You have no choice but to improve public health, and you're doing it on a scale much larger than the one-on-one interactions of a physician. If I were to go back to school, that's the degree I'd get.

And most physicians are not that interested in science. Most pre-meds grudgingly complete the science coursework because they have to, not because they love science.

SHOULD I GO TO MEDICAL SCHOOL?

A medical student on leave

Great blog post that really paints a clearer picture of the medical profession. I have read multiple blogs regarding whether to go into medicine or to actually leave the profession.

I found this blog while I was searching for reasons to drop out of medical school. I am currently on a leave of absence from medical school, because of similar concerns presented in this blog. What I want to provide is my insight as a current medical student on leave.

Before I entered medical school, I had reservations primarily due to financial concerns. I did not go into medical school thinking about how much money I will make. In fact, I calculated the future financial outcome if I continued on with becoming a physician.

In the end, I would pay off my medical school debt in my late-40s/early-50s with little to no savings until then. The values I got were based on $300,000 loan with 6-8% interest, 4 year $50,000 residency pay, and $200,000 post-residency pay. The numbers seem as if it is manageable, which it is IF you decide to live a single life or your significant other has deep pockets. Also, income tax, malpractice insurance cost, living cost, and the number of hours worked were factored in to my calculations.

Another med student on leave

Even after my calculations, I decided to matriculate into medical school, because I felt the financial sacrifices were well worth the opportunity to become a physician. After my time

SHOULD I GO TO MEDICAL SCHOOL?

in medical school and researching more about the US healthcare system and pharmaceutical/biotech industry, you can say I've become disenchanted with the profession. The system is broken and will continue to get worse before improving.

I believe I went into medical school with such optimism that it became idealistic. Young, blind ambition is strong. I thought that I could become a leader for change, but if I am working 80-100 hours/week and worrying about the amount of loans I have to pay off and practicing defensive medicine, I wouldn't be able to practice medicine the way I envisioned.

Another important factor to consider: what do you want out of life? Are family and friends an important part of your life? If they are, be prepared to leave them when pursuing medicine. Medical school alone has narrowed my social interactions to just my fellow classmates and colleagues. Talking about medicine 24/7 does get old quickly.

Which leads to another issue in medicine: if you are a creative individual, medicine will suck it right out of you regardless of how hard you try to maintain it. Prior to medical school, I enjoyed design but deciding between drawing, food or sleep isn't difficult after being awake for 32+ hours.

If you have the financial (i.e. not loans) and/or social (i.e. family and friends) support to pursue medicine, then go for it if that is all you want and/or you cannot, I repeat, *cannot do anything else with your life*. The added stress associated with loans and a failing system just isn't a great combination. That is why I decided to take a year off to explore other opportunities for me that will allow me to wake up everyday contributing positively to society without the excessive burdens that our current healthcare system places on physicians.

Will I return to medical school and continue into residency? Maybe, but for now I have 1 year to find my niche in this world.

SHOULD I GO TO MEDICAL SCHOOL?

Funny, but also really not funny

I'm currently a student at a well-ranked U.S. medical school. Although this article is humorous, it is *not* a joke. It is the absolute truth. Anyone outside the seemingly transparent walls of this bubble is naturally going to misinterpret it. I mean, the author must seem so cynical and ungrateful! There are people all over the world in worse situations, suffering from poverty and various illnesses.

I'm not reducing the gravity of other situations that may appear worse, but there is something equally if not more horrible that comes with the disillusionment one experiences as a physician-to-be. You see the world for what it truly is, and it is absolutely hideous. You see yourself for who you truly are, and you have to face that every single day — most days, that's also hideous.

The realization that you will never reach the top of any mountain, but that you are under mountains upon mountains upon mountains… it's an unfortunate one. This author is not being sarcastic; he is being honest. I've said the same things to individuals wondering whether or not to pursue a career in medicine, not because I think the profession is lame (it's quite the opposite and extremely honorable), but because I truly don't think it is where he or she will find an ounce of happiness without the adequate amount of stubbornness.

A long time ago, I might have responded to this article entirely differently or maybe with ridiculous tears welling up in my eyes. Now I just read it with amusement, accompanied by the dullness of acceptance. Because as it turns out, that's where I am in the stages of grief regarding the loss of my life

SHOULD I GO TO MEDICAL SCHOOL?

(or, at least the "life" that we envision) to this immense pursuit.

SHOULD I GO TO MEDICAL SCHOOL?

The emotional burden of doctorhood

There are people who are genuinely happy in medicine, but those are the exceptions rather than the rule. There are surveys that consistently show that greater than 50% of physicians would choose another profession if given the opportunity.

As a current third-year student at a well-known American med school, I feel as though part of the problem is the way that the profession has been touted by previous generations and portrayed in the media. It isn't the physical demands of the work, the intellectual demands (though they are vast and at times overwhelming) or even the expense that breaks people down. It is the emotional demands and the constant necessity to live up to the societal image of what a doctor is supposed to be: totally compassionate at all times, unfailingly well-informed in every situation (more realistic in the 50s when we had about 1/20th the information to master), and completely without emotion under pressure.
Needless to say, living up to these expectations is entirely unrealistic no matter how hard you work. And yet, the field is only open to individuals with the kind of work ethic that will never relinquish the notion that they have to be perfect.

In other words, medicine can never be just a job – it simply carries too many societal expectations. You work a ton of hours as an investment banker, lawyer, etc. but it ends when you leave the office (generalization, I know). Moreover, if you're a shitty banker, you move on without having let anyone down but yourself. If you're a shitty doctor, you let down yourself, your overbearing parents who likely pushed you into the field, your patients, and, most importantly, society in general. That's a hell of a lot of pressure, and we aren't compensated nearly enough to balance that scale.

SHOULD I GO TO MEDICAL SCHOOL?

The regret of the MS4

I am so sad I did not read this article 5 years ago when I decided to go into med school without giving it much of a thought. Since both my parents are doctors, and I didn't really know what else to do. After these 5 years, I always felt like I was the ogre of my class, hating the bad aspects of being in med school, but certainly, we are on the same page.

Actually, your article is dead on. I laughed and also a little tear might have escaped while reading it because it is so unfortunately accurate. I also am thinking about finishing med school and not studying a specialty nor practicing, because of exactly the points you mentioned above.

My advice to people who are *not sure* if they should study medicine, *do not* study medicine. Only do it if you are literally 100% *sure* and it is your lifelong dream and really *cannot* imagine yourself *not* being a doctor.

Against Medical School: The Practitioners

SHOULD I GO TO MEDICAL SCHOOL?

I am not a discount shoe store

The main reason I went into orthopaedic surgery is because late in med school, I realized that I hated sick people. Not the patients themselves, but the fact that you could work and work and work and at the end of the day you just hoped they were healthy enough to drag themselves out the front door (and come back in on someone else's call). At least in ortho, I admit fully I'm an over-trained mechanic, but dammit, my patients leave at some reasonable time.

Last note, what bullshit is it that your plumber can charge whatever he wants to unclog your drain, but if I replace both knees the insurance companies automatically take 50% off the second. What am I, a fucking discount shoe store?

SHOULD I GO TO MEDICAL SCHOOL?

The clear-eyed orthopedist

I'm a 50 year old orthopedic surgeon. I'm busy, successful, and like going to work.

I believe that most of the points made by Dr Binazir are absolutely correct, though. For those that have commented that he is overly cynical, and perhaps not cut out to be a physician, I would disagree. It's unusual that an individual gets through that much education without "drinking the Kool-Aid." I know of only one or two others that chose not to do a residency.

Sleep, relationships and normal life are lost during training. Debt accumulates. It's not that friends abandon young physicians, it's just that they are never seen. Oddly, many physicians are not aware of what their future practices will be like, and feel underpaid and unloved by their patients.

While it was a good career path for me, it has been difficult in a way I hadn't imagined when I started. There are many interesting and satisfying professions that don't demand your soul in the way that medicine must. I haven't encouraged my children to attend medical school.

SHOULD I GO TO MEDICAL SCHOOL?

The internist's mixed bag

I am a physician in practice in internal medicine for about 10 years. Though I spend the vast majority of my day complaining about how much medicine sucks, I will try to give a balanced and reasoned opinion in case anyone who is considering going into it is reading

First the good news. It is a pretty stable field. Despite probably some changes coming up, I was never in fear of losing my job, pretty much no matter what the economy did. In general, you can practice just about anywhere in the country, from rural to city to suburb, though certain subspecialties may only be practical at major urban medical centers.

While the prestige is definitely not what it used to be, I think most people are still impressed by physicians and they are still generally respected. While the compensation is not what it should be relative to some other fields and most physicians could make more doing something else with the time and years of training they put into it, you can still make a very comfortable living. Also there are a handful of patients I have grown very close to and really enjoy seeing and know they truly appreciate my efforts for them.

The downside: While I do not think you definitely lose friends, it is hard to maintain the same relationship you had with friends and family before. I can't describe the sadness, and loneliness I felt as a resident driving in to work on Christmas morning at 6:00am, seeing no one else on the roads, and knowing I was going to be there for at least 36 straight hours.

SHOULD I GO TO MEDICAL SCHOOL?

Also, you rarely help people. The vast majority of my day is spent seeing people with colds, minor aches and pains and things that really do not need to see a doctor. While I have helped some people and maybe even saved a life or two, that is exceedingly rare and probably outnumbered by the times I have made a mistake (all physicians make mistakes). Most of the time I am treating chronic medical problems like diabetes or high blood pressure that probably help the patient in the long run, but the immediate satisfaction is not there. And for every appreciative nice patient, it seems like there are 5 others who are opiate-addicted, overly demanding and have unrealistic expectations.

SHOULD I GO TO MEDICAL SCHOOL?

The dangers of idealization

I'm an MD nearly out of residency and it's been tough living the reality of each of these truths. I did not choose medicine for the stated in the essay. In my case, there were some hefty family obligations involved, the academic attainability of the position, encouragement of non-medical people around me, and the promise of a stable well-paying job (don't judge).
Here were some thoughts I had at the time that I now know were warning signs of future disgruntlement to come:

"I should do it because it's honorable helping people, contributing to the community, which are good things to do with your life, right?"
"I like learning, and any knowledge learned is good."
"It's a job just like any other job; obviously you won't love every part of it."

If you find yourself abstracting or idealizing the profession to justify going into it, for your own good don't do it.

When it comes down to it, it's not about abstract ideals but instead being able to live with daily reality, which includes constant, high volume interaction with lots of people both pleasant and extremely unpleasant (do you enjoy customer service? a lot of it?), responsibilities where the consequence of a mistake is death or bodily harm, very high patient expectations, overtime as the rule, and lack of partition between your personal life and work.

There's no judgment upon your character if you don't agree with living like this. I'd advise you to pick something else though, or risk being unhappy.

SHOULD I GO TO MEDICAL SCHOOL?

This is how you lose yourself

Indeed, *The House of God* – like no other book – tells the true horrors that must be suffered in the journey from civilian to physician. At one point while on the verge of a breakdown, our protagonist proclaims, "They are trying to kill me!" The inevitable and constant medical complications that can happen at any moment without warning and completely take over your life for untold hours to come: spike a fever, throw a blood clot, infect a port, fall and break a hip or bang out a subdural hematoma. It does *really and truly* feel like you are under assault by your patients, that little by little your patients are trying to destroy you.

But to go back to an earlier point, a very REAL fact about what happens to you when you put on that white coat the first day of medical school:

At the ceremony of the Hippocratic oath, a senior physician warned us that we were entering a new community and that over time the same experiences that would bind us to our colleagues would begin to alienate us from our old communities – friends, families, lovers, etc. Of course, I dismissed this as hyperbole even as I enjoyed the romantic fantasies of radical transformation it evoked. And yet one day years later I woke up to the sudden realization – *it was all true!*

Dr. Binazir's point that the doctors-in-training would gradually lose all of their friends from before medical school is no exaggeration or metaphor. One-by-one, little by little, those tight bonds begin to loosen. Phone calls, letters, emails get slow or no responses. Invitations are repeatedly declined due to a test (in 2 weeks…) and like the phone calls gradually diminish. They *know* they are not going to reach you on the phone, they *know* you are not going to be available to have a drink or go to a party and that when you do make it you are only half there either because you are exhausted or too preoccupied with classes or patients. It stops.

Not out of any vindictiveness or anger or punishment but rather out of resignation and acceptance. It stops occurring to them to call or to invite you along. You have stopped being relevant. Your relationship has become something from the past…a fossil…because it stopped growing, it shrank and became ossified.

Medicine takes over your life, your body, mind and spirit. All of those interests, passions, hobbies, dreams of your youth, they get pushed aside, placed on the shelf, waiting for things to calm down or some semblance of a life to come back to you. There will be moments of longing, pangs of regret, belief in a future that will be different.

But medicine never, ever stops. You have given up for good the possibility of not being responsible; too many people depend on you to ever feel free. And those dreams, those other parts of yourself that were so valuable and so deeply valued, they grow old and brittle and rusted by neglect. Only the strongest and most disciplined among us can ever achieve that holy grail of balance.

You cannot possibly comprehend beforehand what medicine is going to do to you. You will never ever be the same again. You gain this power and privilege, you gain the deep satisfaction of meaningful work and a life's purpose, but you *lose* so much of yourself, you are left as a kind of half person rattling around inside this *role*, this *function* for others. I can't imagine giving it up or giving up having the journey of

SHOULD I GO TO MEDICAL SCHOOL?

becoming a doctor, but I also feel that I have been damaged by it, by medicine, medical school, residency, daily medical practice, etc. Perhaps beyond repair.

SHOULD I GO TO MEDICAL SCHOOL?

The suicide rate

One thing I would like to add (which is sort of mentioned in another comment) is that one big health hazard is suicide: doctors have very high suicide rates not just in US. Base rate of attempts is bad enough in itself, but unfortunately doctors are also very able (due to training etc) to succeed in attempts.

SHOULD I GO TO MEDICAL SCHOOL?

Getting out before it was too late

I was in my 4th year of surgical residency when my body just gave out. I had already been turned into a horrid wench by years and years of abuse and exhaustion. I was suicidal at the time, just hadn't had the courage to go through with the act of killing myself quite yet. While at the time I was devastated–I'd wanted to be a doctor since I was a little girl–I am now so very very grateful.

Interestingly, I had dinner with a former fellow resident a few months ago. She was taking her oral boards, had been practicing in a rural community for a year, had a house, etc. I was floored when she said that she was jealous of me. She already feels trapped and miserable but sees no way out.

I have since switched my practice to acupuncture and medicinal herbs (with a little primary care here and there). My income is no where near what it would be as a surgeon, but I have my life back. I am not angry at the world anymore. I am a whole person again. I am grateful that I sustained the injuries that drove me out of surgical residency. I don't hate people anymore and can take my time in complementary and alternative medicine that I *never* could in medical school or residency.

Although I agree with the comments above that knowledge is never wasted and that there are wonderful reasons to go into medicine, I have to say I wouldn't wish the things that happened to me on any other human being. It was a cruel, cruel process and slowly bludgeons every ounce of humanity out of you. If you are considering applying to medical school, please consider very carefully and weigh the risks because the benefits are not, in my opinion, worth the costs.

SHOULD I GO TO MEDICAL SCHOOL?

SHOULD I GO TO MEDICAL SCHOOL?

The trauma of trauma surgery

The key point being one should not go into medicine except if there is no other possible thing in life that would provide you the satisfaction you would get doing this job. To do that you will sacrifice the best years or your life, your health, your family, and friends. To an extent you would not fathom before hand, and that no one else except those that have been thru it might understand.

The other points though are *all* valid.

I did 9 years of training including general surgery and fellowship training. Most of that was prior to certain work hour changes. Mostly working 80-130 hours a week. Missing all holidays.

The relationships you had with friends — gone. You only come in contact with folks from work.

I can count the times I have seen members of my family over that period on one hand.

I have 300k in debt don't own a house, have a very old car, and no retirement savings. Post training I make barely enough to pay for the loans that I have.

That being said in my field, I see the direct result of the acts that I do. I can physically make a difference in someones life. I practice trauma surgery and critical care medicine, and without the direct intervention of myself or my colleagues, the majority of my patients would have died or have been crippled for life.

SHOULD I GO TO MEDICAL SCHOOL?

I have an MBA in finance, and most of my business school classmates will retire before I make a slight dent in my educational loans. To each his own.

SHOULD I GO TO MEDICAL SCHOOL?

Chief Resident looking for an off-ramp

I'm in my last year of residency. In fact, I'm the chief resident. I love medicine. No, I love the idea of medicine and my 12-year old imagination of how I would save the world as a doctor.

But here I am. Frozen. Stuck 5 months from graduation, the finish line. While all of my colleagues are readily signing job contracts for the next year, 2 years, 10 years, I am nervously spanning the horizon, looking for a detour, an off-ramp, a pothole. Anything but the expected finish and outcome.

And while I may not know yet what I'm going to do next… I am enjoying all the confused looks people get when they ask where I'll be working next year. And I tell them, I'm thinking about becoming a flight attendant.

SHOULD I GO TO MEDICAL SCHOOL?

The disillusioned neurosurgeon

My time as a neurosurgeon has worn me down. My health was suffering and the stress of this profession has made me realize it is not worth it. The patients see you as an enemy somehow instead of someone on their side. They are hoping to find some fault with you in order that they may profit.

I am not encouraging my children to go into medicine. If you have the desire to help people, that's fine, but I would do it through the Peace Corps, not by being a doctor. I have wasted the best years of my life studying as hard as I can to master an unbelievable volume of knowledge and even more studying to stay current, and for what?

I don't even care that we don't make as much money as we did in the past. I just want to get away from the hostility and predatory behavior of the patients and their families. My plan is to become a college professor. It is the only thing I can think to do with this otherwise useless education. If you love life and you want a family life, don't go into medicine.

SHOULD I GO TO MEDICAL SCHOOL?

Is the medical profession sustainable?

I've been practicing internal medicine on and off for 5 years since I finished residency. Having some time off then really allowed me to read up and muse over the financial crisis and overall unsustainable nature of our civilization.

Everything the author says is true, particularly points 5 and 10. Modern physicians don't make nearly as much difference in people's lives as they think they do. And then there are billions of dollars of research to try to prove that some drug or procedure or another gives a 10% decrease in mortality. As if this is meaningful and worth the cost.

Most of my patients are some combination of fat, poor, or old. There's nothing I can do for them. They could be on 10 drugs, and stop all of the drugs tomorrow, and nothing would really change. Antibiotics and insulin do some good, but they too are overprescribed.

And everybody thinks they will live forever! The 22-year old Adonis thinks he will live forever, naturally. But so does the 80-year old with diabetes, COPD, and CHF! And it's my job to try to make that happen.

The incentives in medicine are completely screwed up. We are paid more if we do more, but we can only do more if patients are sicker! There is no incentive to genuinely cure, and no incentive to pull the plug. The incentive is to just keep doing more and more until the system goes bankrupt.

Which it will. This whole thing ends the only way it can: bankruptcy. Just like the banks, just like mismanaged corporations, just like the local, state, and federal governments.

Hospitals and clinics will go bust. There will be no money or resources to run them. And then will we pat ourselves on the back for a job well done?

SHOULD I GO TO MEDICAL SCHOOL?

The MD/PhD's view

This is exactly right and for people who are thinking about going to medical school. As an MD/PhD soon to graduate:
• If you want to make a difference, don't go to medical school unless you absolutely have no idea on how to make a difference.
• If you want to help others, don't go to medical school unless you have no other valuable assets.
• If you want to get rich, don't go to medical school unless you have no other abilities.
• If you are creative, don't go to medical school. Its rules and regulations will stifle the life out of you.
• If you want it to impress others, a million dollar impresses others a lot more.
• If you want security and safety, go to medical school. It will definitely provide you that.

All in all, you get trapped in endless tasks and responsibilities, with no chance for advancement or changing the future.

Medicine is a game and mostly is the NIH of popularity contests, people feeding on each other's ego along with millions of dollars in waste.

To be honest, the only reason why I actually even went to med school was because it offered a redo of college, hopefully to meet someone nice and get married. But then I realized people love money a lot more, while I love helping others.

So the sad reality of this is, I never got what I wanted, nor will I likely and by staying in this field I will never make the same kind of impact on health. After I finish, I probably

SHOULD I GO TO MEDICAL SCHOOL?

won't even do a residency. No matter what your reason is for going into medicine, you will not get what you want out of it.

Ed: The medical profession is probably more stable than that of driving taxis, but it will not necessarily provide you with security or safety. It just exposes you to a different kind of risk and instability. Read on.

SHOULD I GO TO MEDICAL SCHOOL?

The whole story from the UK medic

I've just spent all morning reading this post and comments as I contemplate resigning from my job as an Senior House Officer in the UK [*equivalent to a senior resident in the US - Ed*.].

Sometimes I've been roaring with laughter and nodding in appreciation. I feel so jaded, worn down and stifled as a doctor. I didn't start down the medical path until I was 30, having turned down a place at med school when I was 18 out of fear that it would take over my life. I travelled and taught English across the world and then decided it was time to grow up, and to the delight of my aging parents I announced I was coming home to be a doctor.

Med school was exciting at first. I couldn't believe I'd been given a second chance. I was seriously shocked by the hierarchical nature of the hospital system, the bullying and the arrogance of many of the consultants. I found it frustrating to be talked down to by registrars who were so self-absorbed that they didn't seem to credit me with any life experience, and proceeded to 'teach' (i.e. humiliate), seemingly with the sole purpose of demonstrating their vast learning and acumen. I hated the system but thought once I was through med school, I would feel I could make more of a contribution, and I would never treat students or my juniors in the same way.

As a foundation doctor I certainly did 'contribute', being rushed off my feet, basically picking up the admin work of the consultant who had a vast array of patients who, as director of the hospital, and thus motivated to clear beds at any cost, would stalk around the hospital, discharging patients who "looked too well" to still be there. The number of these who "re-offended" within the ensuing days showed that perhaps he was being a tad hasty. Nevertheless we all know hospital budgets are tight and getting tighter.

I was starting on a set of 4 nights and noticed my heart rate was 100, I was sweating buckets and when I was cannulating a patient the nurse commented that I had the shakes. Suspicious, I got a colleague to take my blood and we sent off for thyroid hormones. Sure enough, TSH was non-existent and free T4 was 5x higher than upper limit of normal. I know you guys in the US use different units for thyroid. Believe me, I was toxic as it gets.

I showed a consultant who put me in touch with an endocrinologist, who told me to take beta blockers and carbimazole [thyroid medication], and come and see him after the nights were over.

Medical nights in a District General Hospital are exhausting enough as it is, but running from one ward to the next with the occasional crash call thrown in, for 12-hour shifts on 4 consecutive nights when I myself was toxic was absolutely exhausting. I even developed angina. However, my work ethic is so strong, I just gritted my teeth and dragged myself through it. I could go on…

I'm now an SHO awaiting September when I am meant to be starting a training programme. As one consultant put it, well done! Keep your nose clean and you'll be a consultant in 8 years.

I'm 38 now. Can I really survive any more of this? My health has deteriorated, I don't have time for my passion (music), hell, I don't even have time to give adequate patient care. Another 8 years of 'keeping my nose clean'?

I'm not sure. The thought of another day makes me feel sick. The irony is that I thought by going in later, with a more mature attitude, I would be able to accept any hardship. I certainly never expected to be one of the moaners. I used to be such a positive person, so full of life. Now I feel like a shell.

SHOULD I GO TO MEDICAL SCHOOL?

Ideals, passion and hard work vs. reality of practice

This article resonates very well with me. Boy I hate the practice of medicine. I love helping people; that's why I went to med school. The idea of figuring out what patients are suffering from and finding solutions to ease their suffering is irresistible. Only that the practice of modern medicine is no longer as simple. I do not know why.

In order to fulfill this dream, one has to put up with all the challenges in the practice. Many who did not go through med school do not understand the concept of modern medical practice. And no, much of the practice is not a necessary evil for the care of patients.

A simple example that is also mentioned in this article is overworked residents and physicians. A tired physician cannot possibly provide better care than a well-rested physician. But yet this idea that physicians must work long hours still persists after numerous studies that show adverse outcomes.

This article explains my frustrations with modern medical practice so well. It will probably continue to hold true until the entire profession changes. Until then, you really need to love the *practice* of medicine (read: not loving patients) to be successful in it.

The essence of medicine is beautiful, but if you ignore the realities of the extremely flawed practice of modern medicine (and whether you can personally take it), you *will* be in a buttload of hurt. This article serves as a very blunt yet necessary warning to those who are considering medicine as a career.

SHOULD I GO TO MEDICAL SCHOOL?

No, your ideals, passion and hard work will not be enough.

SHOULD I GO TO MEDICAL SCHOOL?

The 20-year veteran with a heart of stone

As someone who has practiced medicine for 20 years this article is basically all true, and the real world for medicine is even more vicious at times than the author has said. To succeed in this bizarre medical industrial complex requires real guts, adaptability, and a heart of stone.

I'm doing quite well now, but have lost my hair, my eyesight, and have been divorced twice. If I were to do it all again, I'd probably do dentistry or pharmacy. Or to be honest, I would have gone straight into finance and become a hedge fund manager.

And for all you idealists out there: don't kid yourself. You are not really helping people that often. Medicines are all poisons, most procedures and surgeries are unnecessary, and most people come in with problems caused by their diet and lifestyle and by the time they are seeing you it's already too late. It's all a game, but largely at your expense.

SHOULD I GO TO MEDICAL SCHOOL?

The economics of Australian primary care

To any bright, dedicated young person reading this: Please please please *don't study medicine*. There are 4750+ Australian General Practitioners who are identically trained as the majority of their peers. These 4750+ GPs (primary care doctors) are paid only *half* Medicare from the Australian federal government for the exact same work and responsibility. They are on a pittance.

All Western governments, bureaucrats and media, have it in for the medical profession. This will only increase as the population ages, health budgets strain and medical care continues to consolidate under the banner of corporate conglomerates. In turn this will erode professional independence and standards.

Please do yourself a favour. Save yourself some of *your* life. Save yourself from grief. Study something else.

SHOULD I GO TO MEDICAL SCHOOL?

Medical profession's fine, but the medical professionals…

I love my job. It's scaled down from the ER days to an Urgent Care, but I didn't leave the ER because of the miscreant patients, lousy hours, or insurance hassles. I left because I had to deal with my colleagues. I got tired of having to be the only one who felt duty bound and compelled to work odd hours, weekends, holidays. News flash – it goes with the profession of service. I can perform the roles of many physicians but I couldn't and can't be them all. I don't do surgical orthopedics or neurosurgery or invasive general surgery. I can't attend ICU patients and run an ER simultaneously. I really don't want to reinvent the wheel and learn the complete ins and outs of chronically ill patients and manage their inpatient care when their MD has these insights already. All this "Go to the ER", when they don't feel like making the effort – not because they needed the greater level of care.

Bottom line, I got tired of all colleagues bellyaching about actually having to *work*. Contrary to the rallying cry, none of us are starving or paupers…unless you don't want to work or manage your money correctly or (horrors) live within your means.
Plenty of people work harder than us for a lot less. Many have sacrificed not just their youth like us, but their entire lives to make ends meet.

A lot of this discontent comes from generally discontented people, the grass will always be greener doing or being some place else. So many of my peers say they *hated* the first 2 years of medical school. I thought they were the best years of my life. Made some life-long friends, one of whom genuinely and

SHOULD I GO TO MEDICAL SCHOOL?

literally saved my life once. When we wanted to take a weekend, we agreed to bust our cans and live in the library to get all the studying we needed to get done ahead of time. We had a life outside the course of study—we made it happen. We just chose not to enslave ourselves.

I can take the abuse of society, insurers, government entities— to some degree that has always been there. But the abuse that comes from my less than committed peers is what is truly disheartening. They want the money, but they don't want to absorb themselves into calling like our forebears did. I grew up in a medical household, and my Dad and all his friends worked ungodly hours, but they were in it together whatever their specialties. They socialized and partied and vacationed together. That just doesn't happen as a rule anymore. The collegiality amongst us has eroded to nearly "every man for himself".

By the way, I'm 53 and finished medical school 28 years ago. Plenty of time to get jaded against the medical profession and system. I find myself only getting jaded against medical professionals.

SHOULD I GO TO MEDICAL SCHOOL?

The insecurity of the orthopedist

I told myself I went to medical school because I enjoyed a challenge, but as I reflect upon my choice, I recognize now that I was driven by insecurity. So not only would I seek a career in medicine, but I would become an orthopedic surgeon.

The first dirty secret of medicine is that in order to perform effectively, one must initially go through a process of desensitization, or what might more accurately be described as "dehumanization." Starting as one who was by nature repulsed by cadaveric dissection — so innately disinclined to perform venipuncture upon a classmate, not for fear of blood, but because the thought of inflicting pain was so abhorrent that my hand would shake — it was a remarkable transformation that I would become one who could without hesitation bring a scalpel through live flesh to bone.

The second dirty secret of medicine is we are conditioned by rite of passage through the hell called residency to believe that failure to perform is a sign of personal weakness. It could only have been my insecurity and need for affirmation that I would emerge into private practice and without second thought respond to the middle of the night emergency, labor for hours to reconstruct the self-pay (no pay) trauma victim's open fractures, exposing myself to not only potential blood-borne pathogens, but malpractice liability, and then continue to work through the next day.

Yet at some point in my career, the dwindling reimbursements, the diminishing expressions of patient gratitude, the erosion of my decision-making authority by third-party payers, the constant threat of litigation: my practice was no longer providing solace to my insecurities. I could go on, but sadly I have to get back to work.

SHOULD I GO TO MEDICAL SCHOOL?

The fourth year resident who said sayonara

I quit residency at senior level last year and am very happy with my decision. The premed and med students whom we babysit everyday have no idea about real life. I fully agree with every single sentence in this article. Every doctor I met in my 15 years of medical career told me that they would not become a surgeon/doctor if they could go back in time.

It is a job, just a well-paid job. As they said, only 1% of people can make this amount of money. But they all missed the point; less than 1% of people would like to work so hard, invest so much (time, money, etc) on a fucking job.

SHOULD I GO TO MEDICAL SCHOOL?

OB/GYN wants out

I have been out of residency for 5 years as an OB/GYN and am 35 years old. I want out. Problem is that I am not really qualified for any other job, definitely not a job that would be enough of a salary to pay off my $200,000 in loans.

So like many of the other posters, I am basically stuck, at least until I can pay off the loans. Jobs advertise that call every 5th night offers a "great lifestyle." What planet are these people living on? Delivering babies is fun during medical school and residency but do you really want to be up at 3am doing that for the next 30 years? Then after you are up all night you get to go back to the office and see patients all day long. Then you have to worry about the malpractice on top of it. And frankly, as the initial post mentioned you really just start to dislike the patients since they are the barrier between you and going the hell home.

I was a totally different person when I applied to medical school. I went back and read my personal statement and I literally don't remember that person. You start as a optimistic person who is going to help patients and you come out at the other end a heartless injured person after your soul is sucked out of you by the training and the system.

Ed: Ob/Gyn tends to be one of the tougher specialities. Lots of call, babies don't knock, and the highest malpractice insurance cost of any specialty.

SHOULD I GO TO MEDICAL SCHOOL?

The well-tempered practitioner

I practice, but most of this article rings true for me as well, and I think most of my colleagues would consider me pretty idealistic.

Residency training is mostly cheap labor for hospitals. Working 36 hours straight every third or fourth night (common when I was a resident) saves teaching hospitals from hiring night floats or other coverage. Trying to make any kind of important decision for another human's medical care after you've been up for 24 hours is like trying to do so after several shots of alcohol. Such a schedule does not teach efficiently, endangers patients, and stresses the mental and physical health of physicians. There have been new work rules supposedly limiting residents to 80 hour work weeks, but they are routinely ignored.

Physicians spend most of their time trying to bring order to chaos. Regardless of a physician's specialty, I daresay each was shocked to learn how much time he/she spends basically just trying to simply coax new behaviors in patients — as such, performing at some level as psychiatrists (who I respect greatly - tough work). That's the challenge; everything else is pretty much plumbing.

Either you find that work interesting (and it can be) or you soon get pretty burned out dealing with humans as they are, and they are obviously at their (usually temporary) worst much of the time when they need medical care.

My own colleagues are the best people I know. I still see the driving compassion there on a daily basis, and I think that's true for the great majority of docs. On the other hand, I've met a few physicians who would be happiest in concentration camps performing medical experiments on the inmates.

4. FOR MEDICAL SCHOOL: Medical Students and Practicing Physicians Share Their Thoughts

SHOULD I GO TO MEDICAL SCHOOL?

For Medical School: The Med Students

SHOULD I GO TO MEDICAL SCHOOL?

Julie the MS2

Although I can't say my experience of medical school has been quite like yours (I actually really enjoy it), it's true that I've only been through the first 2 yrs, so who knows what awaits me.

I must say that I'm puzzled by many people's perception that wanting to help people is a good enough reason, in itself, to become a doctor and something that sets the profession apart from others. Although I think it can be a factor that makes the career attractive, I hardly think the profession's unique in being helpful! Nurses, psychologists, social workers, teachers, and countless other professionals are just as helpful and important as doctors. Being a doctor is just one way to be helpful to others and many other things (money, prestige and pleasing parents don't count, of course!) should motivate someone to choose such a demanding career if they are to have any chance at being happy while doing it.

In my opinion, one should consider the job as a whole and think that even while sleep-deprived, even when everyone seems to only be able to talk about all that's wrong with doctors, even when the attending is yelling at you and you've never felt less competent, even when a patient dies and maybe you could have prevented it but didn't, and even when you have to miss a good friend's wedding and your parent's anniversary or your child's birthday because you're scheduled to work, even then *that's* what you want to be doing with your life. If not, you probably won't enjoy it, because all these things are bound to happen. I think the main motivation should just be that it's the career that seems to be the most interesting to you in spite of all that's wrong with it.

SHOULD I GO TO MEDICAL SCHOOL?

Maybe I'll end up regretting going to medical school one day, but I went because I knew that if I didn't, I'd regret not trying it.

SHOULD I GO TO MEDICAL SCHOOL?

Luigi the MS4, point-by-point

Fourth year med student here to offer some counter arguments to each of the points mentioned above:

1) You will lose all the friends you had before medicine: I agree that you will loose many of your "acquaintances" before medicine, but not your "friends." If anything my journey through med school has allowed me to strengthen my true friendships by sharing my stories, hard times, good times, interesting cases, etc. with friends. I now have a better grip on who my true friends before med school were....and they are still plenty. Not to mention, you do develop some great friendships during med school itself, just like any people who go through a challenging time together.

2) You will have difficulty sustaining a relationship and will probably break up with or divorce your current significant other during training: This I absolutely agree with, though for me it is not necessarily a bad thing. I enjoy short term relationships and find girls my age (mid twenties) play with their hair every time they hear I'm in med school. To each his own I guess.

3) You will spend the best years of your life as a sleep-deprived, underpaid slave: You will be sleep deprived, and you will be underpaid. But money really does not sum up what "payment" means. There's something to be said for that feeling you get when you intubate someone and have to take over their respiratory system; for being elbow deep in someone's abdomen during a trauma case; for being the first person in the world to touch a baby.

And while all these can definitely get old after a while, I'd prefer these rewards over a $20,000 bonus any day. [*How*

SHOULD I GO TO MEDICAL SCHOOL?

about a $2,000,000 bonus? Ed.] Because lets face it, you're never going to be hungry, you'll definitely have a middle- to upper-middle class lifestyle, and your job security is second to none.

Oh and don't forget, when you walk in to the hospital cafeteria at 5:30 a.m before rounds to get your coffee, there's someone on the other side of the counter also there at that godforsaken early hour, except they're making $7.25/hr and everyone looks right past them.

4) You will get yourself a job of dubious remuneration: If money is #1 or #2 or your list of life goals, then I agree: do not go into medicine. Remember, even if you make seven digits in medicine and buy that mansion, your neighbor down the road will be in the same neighborhood, his/her kids will go to the same school as your kids, except he/she owns 4 gas stations and 3 pizza places.

5) You will have a job of exceptionally high liability exposure. I do not practice and am not really qualified to talk about this, but I will say that these days as more and more docs work for HMOs or academic centers, your malpractice is covered by the organization, but again I don't know much about this issue. Not a deal maker or breaker to me anyway.

6) You will endanger your health and long-term well-being: I've met some of the most athletic people in my life in med school. About 20 people in my class run marathons, and the rest regularly work out. I myself have lost weight since starting school (admittedly because of a lack of time to eat, but that's ok, as humans we were not meant to eat this much anyway). To argue that not having time to eat is frustrating and decreases your quality of life is one thing, but to say it actually

SHOULD I GO TO MEDICAL SCHOOL?

makes your unhealthy is another. Although one can't deny the sleep deprivation and its effects on the immune system.

7) You will not have time to care for patients as well as you want to: For most fields in medicine this rings true. though fields like pathology, radiology, anesthesiology, dermatology, and a few others do fine.

If you can't take care of patients as well as you want to, I think to some extent you have to change your expectations. Just because one enters med school with the naïve view that one can save everyone and listen to them fully, doesn't mean you have to keep this view. Time is limited for everyone, you divide it as best you can, and as long as there's no regrets it's all good to me.

8) You will start to dislike patients — and by extension, people in general: This I have felt. Though after a while I mostly feel sorry for them. regardless, if you are able to have a fulfilling life outside the hospital I think all this becomes more bearable. When I know I have to go home and masturbate instead of having sex, then yeah I get frustrated more easily. But through medicine I've actually become much more comfortable talking to people, reading their body language, and articulating my points.

9) People who do not even know you will start to dislike you: At the end of they day they need you and they know it. They wouldn't come to your office or hospital if it was otherwise.

10) You're not helping people nearly as much as you think: I'm no messiah, and I don't think any of you are either. You do what you can. Don't take yourself so seriously and think you have

SHOULD I GO TO MEDICAL SCHOOL?

to save the world. People are free to fuck up their bodies and minds if they want to.

Anyway, I'm mostly writing this in case any pre-meds are reading the article just so they get another perspective.

SHOULD I GO TO MEDICAL SCHOOL?

Nontraditional MS4 DO student

I'm a 4th year DO student applying to residencies and I'm turning 30 in a month. Yes, for all of you who believe your "prime years" are in your 20s, run and hide from this profession. After graduating with a BS in psychology, I spent 4 years finding myself. I traveled to different parts of the world after saving money working at a hedge fund for 1.5 years. Did I mention I was an administrative assistant in HR, working 14 hr days but making more than either of my blue collar parents?

Had a condo in wealthy southeast Connecticut and bought a car in that short time. I was making *bank*, planning company parties without an unlimited budget and met some wonderful, brilliant people at my job, but it wasn't my calling. I did some part time classes to fulfill my premed requirements and applied to med school. The DO schools looked much more favorably upon students who were a little bit seasoned with life experiences.

The happiest classmates are those who are in their 30s, 40s and even 50s. We have a wonderful "team & family" approach and the majority are never cut-throat like some of the previous posts mentioned. Perhaps you should've explored the programs before jumping into "Prestige University" to get your MD or DO degree.

I would have never appreciated my struggles if I didn't experience other things. For example: after spending 3 months in a 3rd world country (Brazil) at a rural clinic where insurance doesn't exist (for patients or doctors), no one should be complaining about how much we don't get paid. I did do the "make tons of money and buy nice things and party with my friends." If it's your calling, no one, especially a book, will persuade you otherwise.

Yes, most of the things Ali lists above are true for the majority since the majority have only experienced college and never lived it up before diving into the most challenging experience of their lives. I met my boyfriend (current intern hating his life) in med school. We keep each other afloat and find the humor in our humble lives. He is going into anesthesiology and will ultimately be happy with his life since he's generally an optimistic person.

I'm going into Physical medicine and Rehabilitation. It's fulfilling for me to improve the lives of young veterans with traumatic brain injuries and people with spinal cord injuries. They are the most appreciative patients and they even find the humor in life.

Take some time to do other things and explore other avenues. If you are meant to practice medicine, you'll suck it up and make the most of the blessings people tend to overlook.

SHOULD I GO TO MEDICAL SCHOOL?

MS3 and loving it

As a third year medical student, I am sad that this article is getting as much credence as it is. While some of these points may be experienced by individuals at one point or another in their medical career, this is certainly *not* representative of the average person's experience. While I am only a third year, I have made it through many of the gamuts of medical school already — at a top, rigorous institute [*Johns Hopkins, specifically - Ed.*] and strongly disagree with many of the comments. While we may not be able to have the lush lives of some of our peers who entered different tracks, we as future physicians can still enjoy many of the same enjoyable experiences of our era.

Yes, you will certainly lose some college and high school friends throughout medical school — who doesn't?! When each of us moves to a new place, job, career, this is an inevitable outcome. However, I still stay in contact with and see my three best friends twice a year — and we all live on opposite coasts! It's not that hard to pick up a phone on your way to or from the hospital or during one of your breaks on rotation.

Medical school is first and foremost about learning to allocate your time in a way that works for you. *Make* the time to take care of yourself, it's there, trust me! I've actually been to 5 new countries and 7 new US States since coming to medical school — some of these expenses even paid by school! Conferences and projects are always open and available. Find them and take advantage!

While it is certainly rough on some rotations to find hours upon yours to spend with your sig-o, it is not impossible.

SHOULD I GO TO MEDICAL SCHOOL?

Your work load waxes and wanes, and it's all about finding someone who can support you when you need it, and enjoy your free time when you have it. I've been dating a wonderful guy (non med!) for over two years now and our relationship is great. You both have to understand that as busy professionals, you're not going to be that lovey-dovey couple who spends every night making gourmet meals together over candle lit tables. But that doesn't mean you can't have one of those nights every now and then. And it makes it all the more special.

The hours can be tough sometimes, that is true. But what about your finance friends who are also working 12-16 hours a day? And your top firm lawyers who works more hours than I can physically even understand? With the new laws in place, medical students can't even stay past certain times at the hospital — you're forced to go home. But then when you think you can't make it another day, the rotation is over! And you have time off! And you rest and you go back into the new rotation! It doesn't last forever, and it's not like every day is misery. Much of what you do is actually enjoyable (surprise!!) and makes the day fly by.

Many of the other comments rotate around the theme of ingratitude — from patients, from co-workers, etc. While some patients are absolutely awful, why didn't I hear mention of those ones who are great? Who hug you sobbing in joy, after you've told them their baby is going to survive? That you've successfully cured their mother of cancer? For every patient who makes your life a living hell, there are more who are so grateful for all you've done for them. If you've had the opposite experience, did you ever think that you as the student or resident might be doing something wrong to alienate the patients?

SHOULD I GO TO MEDICAL SCHOOL?

To wrap this up, yes, medical school and the medical profession can be extremely difficult at times. This is why not all people are meant to be doctors. Being a doctor can be a wonderful and enlightening career path. It is something I've only had overwhelmingly positive experiences with. I hope that everyone understands there are two sides to any coin, and if you want to help people, then becoming a doctor may be for you. It is something you should consider and weigh carefully because it is a commitment. But it is not *nearly* as bleak as this article makes it out to be.

Ed: It's worth noting that some medical schools are more user-friendly than others.

SHOULD I GO TO MEDICAL SCHOOL?

What's your opportunity cost?

I sense that you're affiliated with Harvard. Your writing reflects that you went to school with and hang around social elites who went to Ivy League schools, and thus could have any job they wanted in finance, banking, law, etc. For them, medicine would be a bad bet: it has a gigantic opportunity cost of these high-paying careers.

For the rest of us, there is no opportunity cost. Top law schools (the schools you need to attend to get into big law), investment banking firms, etc, they don't want people who went to third-tier state schools. For us, those high-paying careers are not accessible. Medicine is accessible, because med schools don't care about where you went to college.

Basically, for a Harvard grad, medicine is a bad bet because Harvard can get him a great job on Wall Street. For a state school grad, medicine is still a great choice because he doesn't have any other high-paying jobs accessible to him.

I will start med school this August, and I will always remember to tell myself this: "For me, the opportunity cost of going to medical school was a future of uncertain employment and sub-$50K jobs."

SHOULD I GO TO MEDICAL SCHOOL?

It's all about the right fit

I belonged to a pre-medical school sorority, where we all joined because we wanted to support each other in becoming doctors. While we were all stressed, some of us were completely miserable and for some, the pressure got to be too much. They struggled for a long time with the decision to quit the med school path. Once some of them made that simple choice, I was completely amazed at the sense of relief and peace that they exuded immediately afterward. This was the most positive and happiest I had ever known them to be! It was obviously a great choice for them and I am happy that they figured out what they wanted in time!

Today, I have classmates that are seriously questioning their decision. They have such disdain for the whole process, but they owe $125,000+ so they don't see a way out but to graduate. I hear them say this all the time and I would hate to have them treat me, or anyone I knew! It would have been great for them to read this post so that they would know earlier what they were getting into. Many of them are really young, come to med school with credit problems, no idea of what responsibility, or what work ethic really means, and are sorely disappointed with what they find.

Some friends I have, knew what they wanted, were going for it, would be great doctors, accumulated a lot of debt in the process, but weren't allowed to finish med school.

I think all of us in med school question our decision from time-to-time (depending on the week), but I feel for some of us, there is absolutely nothing else we can imagine doing in life when it comes down to it. There are few things in life that are as wonderful as walking into a room and seeing a family have their child back. That moment when we forget just for a moment all the chaos and suffering in the world, and instead feel overwhelmed with joy at seeing one little positive thing that is finally smiling and giggling back at us after being so seriously sick! Yes there are some people who aren't the best parents, but they are being the best person they know how to be. Some of them have a longer way to go than others, but I feel up to the challenge to try and help when I can! This profession is the icing on the cake for me and I am loving every minute of it!

I am $310,000+ debt solely due to my education, still have 1.5 more years of med school (at the tune of $80,000/year) plus 3 more years of my pediatrics residency (I think we start at $45,000 and have to start paying back loans), but I feel so lucky to get to do medicine everyday. I recognize I am a slave for the rest of my life (paying back the loans until I die), but luckily I have my partner who pays off the home we share, so that I can focus on learning and then later volunteering my medical knowledge (part-time-40 hours) to the communities that need me.

The other part of my life that I will enjoy is being with my partner, watching our children grow, having us travel to help out under-developed nations and maybe even vacation somewhere nice sometime. I am living the life I have always dreamed of. I wish I had more of a social life, but the good news is that although I don't have many friends anymore, the ones I do have are the ones I know are truly there for me — no matter what!

I wish those people who aren't sure what they want would please take the time to consider what kind of opportunities they are taking from someone else who really wants and

SHOULD I GO TO MEDICAL SCHOOL?

deserves to be here! There are some really good future doctors out there and our communities could sure use them! Good luck in finding your path!

For Medical School: The Practitioners

SHOULD I GO TO MEDICAL SCHOOL?

The minuses *and* the pluses
Dr Binazir writes realistically about large problems and difficulties in the medical profession. However, for everyone who has read this, realize that there are just as many positive reasons why you should go to medical school and become a doctor.

There are pros and cons to every decision, and the grass always seems greener on the other side, but at the end of the day, you have to realize your own personal values and priorities and choose according to them. For some people, medicine presents a unique set of challenges that has personally and financially rewarding aspects. Others were meant to do other great things.

SHOULD I GO TO MEDICAL SCHOOL?

The radiologist living large

I am a diagnostic radiologist. Med school was tough but it was not the end of the world. I had fun in med school with a positive attitude. Got laid all the time, made great friends. My attitude is what helped me be successful in my goals. Now I make around $440,000 a year, take a lot of vacations. Malpractice insurance is a pain but it's not terrible. My only regret is being away from family for so long. Other than that, I am straight up doing it right now.

Ed: For those of you who read Samuel Shem's immortal classic The House of God, you're aware that some specialities suck much less than others. In the book, they are called NPC specialties — no patient care. And they are "six and only six": Rays (radiology), Gas (anesthesiology), Path (pathology), Ophthalmology, Psychiatry, and Dermatology. Of those six, Derm, Ophtho and Rays are a cut above. Med students have caught on — hence, the stringent requirements for scoring a residency in one of those specialities.

SHOULD I GO TO MEDICAL SCHOOL?

The ex-nurse

I recently was contacted by someone asking about going to medical school. Like me, this person was a nurse and thinking about going back to school.

I went to medical school after being a nurse for 8 years. I had always wanted to be a doctor and really couldn't see myself not doing it. So here is the up side to all of this: I love my job. I love everything about it. I love the patients, I love the people I work with.

Here is more upside: I have been married for over 20 years (and I still love my husband). I have six kids, and so far they seem okay.

I have friends and a life. I like to swim, run, play tennis, play golf and watch my kids activities.

More good stuff: I make a really good living. I make more money than I ever expected to make.

Better: My student loans weren't so bad because I went to a state school for medical school. I had three kids when I started school and had another in med school, another during residency and then my last one when I was an attending. More: I was a chief resident with five kids — and I loved it.

So for all you naysayers: If you really, really, really want to be a doctor, go for it. Not a day goes by that I regret my decision. You can have relationships and a life. You just have to remember all the people who helped you get to where you are. My husband was my biggest fan. And I will never ever be able to thank him enough for encouraging me to go to school. He never once said don't do it.

P.S. My oldest daughter is considering medical school…I told her "good for you!"

Ed: Good for her! Please note that this person was a) a nontraditional student (over 30 years old) b) had pre-existing social support in the form of a husband and c) already figured out she liked taking care of patients in her 8 years as a nurse. Your mileage may vary.

SHOULD I GO TO MEDICAL SCHOOL?

The secret trapdoor to debt-free med school

I finished medical school (MD/PhD) in 2003, residency/fellowship in 2008, and in practice in academia for a few years now, and none of what he wrote is true, or at least, universally true. Medical school wasn't that bad. I met my wife during that time, and had a lot of fun. Hours were bad periodically, but only on certain rotations, and I now have a job with regular hours, and I don't have any debt.

The secret? I'm a pathologist, and the federal government paid for medical school through the Medical Scientist Training Program (i.e. I got paid to go to medical school). The path to neurosurgery is similar to what he wrote, but all of medicine does not equal neurosurgery. There are plenty of routes through the training that don't require one to kill one's self, and it's not fair to say so.

And, I might have to amend one thing. He's pretty close about the money thing. You are not paid nearly enough in academia for spending your 20s in school and working up. No one starves in medicine, but you may not get paid enough to save effectively for sending kids to college if you stay in academics. Private practice gets you several*fold* more money, not just a percentage more.

Ed: The MSTP gives you a full-ride scholarship for med school and a PhD, plus a stipend. It's not for everyone, but if you're planning on becoming a biomedical scientist, it's a great deal. Also, note that pathology is the ultimate NPC specialty, in the sense that your patients do not complain. Ever.

SHOULD I GO TO MEDICAL SCHOOL?

The small-town family practitioner

I totally agree with your evaluation of medical school experience. I feel that it completely raped my soul, to the point that I have lost who I was. Since then, I have recovered, as my residency was great and now that I am working, I am my own boss and can decide how much or little I want to work. The quarter million dollar student debt does suck, but I am slowly paying it off.

Prior to going into medical school, I was a teacher and found that job much more difficult than being a doctor. It wasn't the teaching, but the bureaucracy was deadly. Now as a family doctor, I have control over my time and work, because I am my own boss. I also have the ability to change my job over time, if I feel I am getting bored. Right now, I deliver babies, follow my own inpatients in the hospital (I live in a small city where family doctors have admitting privileges in hospitals), do surgical assists. If I feel I need a new challenge, I can get additional training in palliative care, GP oncology, geriatrics, or anything else that is required in my community and challenge myself that way. It is a fabulous job! Yes, medical school sucks, but in hindsight, it was worth it for me.

Ed: A lot of the happy stories seem to come from small-town docs.

SHOULD I GO TO MEDICAL SCHOOL?

The neurosurgery resident

The decision to pursue medicine, like all important decisions, is a personal one. The author enumerates many of the well-known and thoroughly-discussed arguments against pursuing an MD. The opportunity cost of pre-medical training, 4 years of medical school, 3-7+ years of residency and/or fellowship, are obviously large. Too large for him.

Other individuals who choose this path find the benefits of treating and comforting the sick, of obtaining their trust and rarely, of curing illness are much greater than what he grants. My experience has been different.

I am four years into an neurosurgery residency with 3 left (and possibly a year or two of fellowship thereafter). However, although there are drawbacks and downsides, I enjoy my job. It is challenging, rewarding and unique. Occasionally, I can make a profound difference in someone's life. Each individual must decide for himself.

SHOULD I GO TO MEDICAL SCHOOL?

The mommy surgeon

There's no such thing as having it all. Everyone makes sacrifices, and you just have to pick which ones are worth making. I actually started out in the pharmaceutical industry, and otherwise probably would not have gone to medical school. It just wasn't enough. But if I hadn't, I would probably be a VP by now, and miserable.

Med school was a great time, and I miss those friends terribly. Almost as much as my college friends. Most friendships do fade, and you can't make those reunions like you want to. But you pick those one or two special ones and dedicate your energy to those. Here's the thing: that happens to everyone as we get sucked into "real life." You think that Mr. Investment Banker at Goldman working 70 hours a week with two kids, wife, and house in the Hamptons is out partying it up with his college buddies? There's no such thing as having it all.

Residency was the second best time of my life. Nothing beats college. Ever. But those people mean more to me than almost anyone outside of my family. Because we became family. We helped each other through everything – dying patients, unruly attending physicians, OR mishaps, 15 gunshots in one night. And we laughed together like I never thought possible. Residency graduation was the hardest thing ever.

I had a child in the middle of surgical residency. The timing was as right as I thought it could be. But he was four when I graduated, and I'm not quite sure how that happened. I hope I haven't caused too much damage. But now, in breast cancer fellowship, I'm doing my best to make it up to him. It's been a long, exhausting road, but my life is actually getting back to "normal" now. I think he's in shock that I'm home every

SHOULD I GO TO MEDICAL SCHOOL?

night and we have breakfast together most mornings. He's getting to know his mommy again.

We all have pain, medicine or not. You can't have it all. But I'm well on the way to getting most of it back.

Ed: Did you get that part about missing the first four years of her kid's life? Jeebus, man. Also, please note that surgeons are a different breed of human being altogether. If you're hell-bent on becoming a surgeon, then stop reading this book immediately, because nothing we say is going to make a difference.

SHOULD I GO TO MEDICAL SCHOOL?

The soldiering general surgeon

I'm a general surgeon in my mid 40's (married to a pediatrician, two kids). My daughter asked me the other night: "Daddy, what is your dream job?" I replied: "I have my dream job." I can't imagine doing anything else. I believe I make a difference in peoples' lives every day. I was an Army Officer before going to medical school, so I even enjoyed classes, ward rotations etc. Even the sleep deprivation wasn't too bad. I wasn't shot at once. Residency was challenging, but just ask anyone else today working two or three jobs about that.

It's all a matter of perspective. I recently read *Mao's Last Dancer*. Amazing amount of hard work, sacrifice and ultimately some lucky breaks to become successful. Everyone today seems to expect success without hard work and sacrifice. Yes, some I-bankers make ridiculous money. I don't think this is the norm. Is this a generational or cultural thing that we expect everything to be handed to us on a silver platter? Physicians may not have it great, but they have it pretty good. And it could be a whole lot worse (and may soon be). Perhaps our national affluence is too much of a hurdle to overcome.

My advice: spend time with a community physician, or better yet, several community physicians. Most medical schools now require this. For the past two years, I have mentored undergraduate pre-meds doing rotations to satisfy this requirement. While some students come from medical families, none really has any idea about what we do on a day to day basis. Most (not all) are enthralled with the experience.

SHOULD I GO TO MEDICAL SCHOOL?

In closing, I do agree with Ali's closing comment. If you can see yourself doing something else besides medicine, you should probably do that. Medicine is a demanding mistress with few exit points once you get started.

Ed: Once again, a non-traditional medical student. Knew what he was getting himself into. Appreciated not getting shot at.

SHOULD I GO TO MEDICAL SCHOOL?

Good enough for this MD/PhD

I read this article when I was premed and you terrified me. But I knew I wanted to medicine for the patient relationships. I am an Ob/Gyn, so I know all about malpractice and how bad insurance sucks; and I am the queen of sleep deprivation. However, I have plenty of time for family and friends. Residency was rough but Med School was okay. I now also teach at NYU and I love it. It made it all worth it.

Sometimes I wonder if I should've skipped med school and just done the PhD for free and taught. However, I do like my patient relationships. Except for the ones that sue me, my patients love me and treat me with respect. I do not resent humans as you said. I appreciate them and life more by being a doctor.

I think being a doctor alone is stressful. I think we are underpaid. However, once I added teaching, I had more time and pleasure for everything in my life. Med school loans can easily be paid off. Honestly, everyone in my old practice takes ski trips and Europe trips every year.

My only regret is that I feel like I wasted my prime. I would've preferred med school not to eat up my 20s. Also I would suggest going to med school in a place you love. I attended NYU and it made med school more pleasant. However, it did add significantly to my debt (which I paid off in 7 years) but it was stressful during med school. Perhaps wait until residency to move to New York City if you are considering.

SHOULD I GO TO MEDICAL SCHOOL?

Ed: I'm just going to note that there are only so many jobs in the world where getting sued by your customers — whom you were trying to heal, mind you — is considered completely normal.

SHOULD I GO TO MEDICAL SCHOOL?

It's a marathon, not a sprint

In the trenches of surgical residency (arguably the most intense part of one's medical career) and living it. Every day is unpredictable and challenging and high stakes, but every day I learn something new and that constant stimulation is something I don't think I would get in any other field. Someone had a comment about seeing the forest through the trees and that is the key to survival in medicine. You have to see the whole patient but you also have to picture your future job as an attending – which is nothing like medical school or residency.

Not only did I make more friends in these past 7 years of school and training (both in and outside of medicine), but I developed some very deep lasting relationships. With the Internet and FaceTime its easier to keep in touch than ever.

It is a marathon, and it's not for everyone, but if you persevere you can accomplish something pretty amazing.

SHOULD I GO TO MEDICAL SCHOOL?

The view from sunny Portugal

I'm a Portuguese med student, and here things are very very different in many ways.

First, we pay 1.000€ (roughly $1200USD) per year of med school, so I have no idea of what being in debt is, even though I'm a fifth year (here med school is 6 years).

Second, here healthcare is universal, which means no insurance companies. Why would you pay taxes *and* a private insurance? Why not pay a little more taxes and have health for everyone? You take out an intermediary that only sees profit, and the "deal" is made between two entities committed to helping people, and not profit. They are the government: paying for health costs, and the hospitals: providing the health services.

Third, we get paid very well when compared to other people here.

Fourth, we have no lawyers interested in ruining doctors' lives with lawsuits. Malpractice cases are handled by the medical boards, and all is done to improve care and minimize the damage to the patient. Although it happens sometimes, the main goal is not to punish the doctor if he made an honest mistake. Deliberate mistakes and abuses are highly penalized.

Fifth we don't work so much as American doctors I think. It depends on specialties, but most doctors do one 24h shift a week, and have two days off (one of them in the weekend and the other one during the week, usually the day after a 24h shift).

SHOULD I GO TO MEDICAL SCHOOL?

But above all of this, those reasons are why you don't like medicine, not why everyone should hate it. I still think it's the right path for me, and I could see myself doing a lot of other things. Also, there are no doctors in my family, and I have never felt any kind of pressure from my parents to become a doctor.

But what you call grueling I call challenging. I love to change someone's life by simply making it crystal clear that if they don't do what they're told they will die earlier. Explaining the disease, how it affects the individual, and how it can be cured or treated is something I truly enjoy.

When you're interviewing someone in the ER and the puzzle starts to come together and you begin to predict the patient's answers because you already have a strong suspicion is a feeling of accomplishment like none other to a very curious and engaged mind.

When you get to talk to a family and say that their loved one has gone through this and that, but they'll make a recovery, having someone bring you a bottle of wine because you helped them understand how to properly take their meds and now they feel like a new person (yes, it has happened to me more than once!) *greatly* outweighs all the efforts, all the long hours, all the sleep deprivation, all the studying and unrecognized efforts. It's just worth it!

But since this is all subjective; it could be worth it for me and not for you. It's *my* true calling, and I don't think I'd be so challenged in any other job. Medicine is the perfect balance between intellectual challenge, good-doing, and human interaction.

SHOULD I GO TO MEDICAL SCHOOL?

Having said that, we do only live once, so I'm choosing a specialty that will allow me to have a family and keep my friends, and that pays well. No general surgery for me.

I'd also like to say that if you don't like how medicine is practiced, *you're the perfect person to go into medicine*!! You can change things.

Your time with your patients is yours, you're the one setting the tone, and driving the interview, so medicine is one of the few professions where one individual can make a huge difference in other people's lives.

Again, if you think things should change, then come on in and change them. It's really easy to stand back and say "Because I don't like how it's done, I'm not joining", but it's a lot harder and fulfilling to say "You know what? I don't like how that's done, and I can see a number of ways it could be done differently, so I'm gonna join in and change things!"

If you applied that mentality to other things, you'd be alone inside a cave. How many times do you not like how your family does family, or how your school does schooling, or how your friends do friendship? Do you give up, or demand more from them and continue loving them? Call me idealistic, but that's how I view things.

SHOULD I GO TO MEDICAL SCHOOL?

Christa, the resident who makes a difference

The article makes all excellent and true points. That being said, there is *nothing* in the world better than the feeling of making a difference in the life and health of another. The days I leave the hospital knowing that simply by my being there, there is someone alive who wouldn't have been (or conversely, someone who is now facing end-of-life with the respect for their wishes that they deserve) — it doesn't get any better than that, folks.

I'm a 3rd yr resident, and while there are so very many times when I agree with everything written in Dr Ali's article, I wouldn't change my job for the world. Don't go into medicine for money (cause you'll make more elsewhere), or respect, or to make someone else happy. There are already too many people like that. Go into medicine because you love it. That way, when you are hating your life and hating the patient in front of you and hating your fellow residents and hating the nurses (and the list goes on), you'll still love your job. Just not at that moment.

SHOULD I GO TO MEDICAL SCHOOL?

Bob the stoic surgeon

Medicine is stressful and taxing in many ways. As a surgeon, I can relate to your references to losing the best years of your life, lost relationships and opportunities. I have seen many of my friends make more money than I will likely earn.

In college, I faced the choice of matriculating into a top law school or go to medical school. There are days I regret my decision. I think people in any profession have such days. More often than not, however, I love what I do. No other profession combines the intellectual satisfaction, manual dexterity, solid pay, job security, social prestige and independence I have.

I don't hate my patients, even on ER nights when I come in a 3 AM to handle something. And I have been able to maintain many of my non-medical friendships. My friends' jobs are boring; they make a ton of money but they crunch numbers and talk about how to "maximize value and arbitrage opportunities."

My radiologist, dermatologist, pathologist, anesthesiologist, ophthalmologist, and ER doctor friends are uniformly happier than I am. My advice to college students considering a career in medicine: It is a long haul, with ups and downs. You will not be worth tens of millions of dollars, but you will be very comfortable. You will achieve a satisfaction and pride in your work that non-medical professionals or mid-levels (NPs, PAs) cannot understand or appreciate.

Regarding Ali's comments regarding innovation and entrepreneurship: I have known many doctors who have started companies or have used their earnings to leverage themselves into other investments. I cannot predict the future or what impact the ACA will have on a still wonderful profession, but I do not regret my decision.

Ed: By now you may have noticed a theme: the speciality you pick makes a huge difference in the quality of your life. More on this coming right up…

SHOULD I GO TO MEDICAL SCHOOL?

Katie, the anesthesiologist who stumbled on happiness

I just wanted to chime in and say that a lot of this depends on specialty choice. I knew I wanted to be a doctor from the time I was in high school, although I briefly became an engineering major as a freshman in college in an attempt to dissuade myself from medical school. That was a bust, since I *hated* engineering. So I switched to microbiology/pre-med and had a truly great time in college.

I know this is hard to believe after reading a lot of the comments here, but I loved med school (the classroom work, most of my rotations, and my amazing friends/fabulous experience in a great city/great boyfriend). The environment at my school (top 5, pass/fail) was really supportive, somewhat from the administration, but mostly from my classmates, many of whom continue to be my closest friends despite the fact that we are scattered all over the country for residency. It was one of the best times in my life.

Somehow I ended up in an anesthesiology elective and realized that I loved critical care and anesthesiology during my third year. Currently, I'm a third year anesthesiology resident in a combined anesthesia/critical care fellowship track. Although I'm tired and don't have the flexibility to randomly go out of town like some of my non-medical friends, and although I definitely don't have the flexible income as a lot of my other friends (grad student boyfriend + residency salary + paying off my loans), I wouldn't trade it for anything.

I have enough time off to go on trips, go to yoga, go to the movies, and live the life I want. And I genuinely love my job. It's intellectually stimulating, fun, provides the opportunity to

SHOULD I GO TO MEDICAL SCHOOL?

meet lots of patients, requires me to use *all* my knowledge of physiology/pharmacology/pathophysiology *all* the time, and my co-workers are uniformly laid-back and interesting.

All that being said, I think I'd hate my life if I was in any other field. I don't know how I got lucky enough to have my teenage idea of doctoring become a reality. But yes, for some of us, it really is what we want and the sacrifices of time and money are worth it.

Also, I should add that I went straight through, which means I'm 29 right now. I went to public school for undergrad without debt thanks to some college money set aside by my late grandparents, and I have about $200K of med school debt that I'm paying off through income-based repayment. And I don't really want to have kids, so that probably helps me to be okay with my lifestyle and financial situation.

Ed: Some recurring themes: A) It makes a big difference if you go to a mellow med school, vs. a user-hostile one. Pass-Fail grading makes a huge difference. B) Choice of specialty matters. C) Not wanting kids is a game-changer if you're female.

SHOULD I GO TO MEDICAL SCHOOL?

Alfredo, the grateful academic physician

I'm the opposite of your medical school dean. I've loved my academic medicine life so my daughter chose medical school and academics as well. We're both very happy. But we both knew the issues you so brilliantly articulated.

Medicine is bad as a business model. Too little power and too much responsibility. Unless, of course, it's the responsibility you crave. The responsibility of taking care of very sick patients, of teaching and passing on the torch and of making new knowledge to move the field. This is its own reward. Add to that the love and devotion of all the young people (especially residents and fellows) who put their careers in your hands. It's all quite a privilege.

Maybe it's also cognitive dissonance. If you put up with crap, it must be worthwhile. Tell that to a mother of a baby who is nothing but work and shows no gratitude. She will tell you that all the bad nights and dirty diapers and anxieties were all part of the best thing she ever did.

Okay, I've been lucky. I've had a great career sheltered in academics. But being surrounded not only by the best and brightest, but by idealists is an amazing joy. So I'll finish by making this point with a metaphor.

When the horrific tsunami hit Thailand and Indonesia, two planes were chartered to fly to Thailand from LAX. One was filled with doctors and nurses eager to help out. The other with lawyers eager to exploit the tragedy. Suppose there was one available stand by seat on each plane. Which plane would you choose? Which group would you choose to spend time with? I'm very glad that I've spent my life with fellow enthusiasts who knew it was a joy and privilege to help patients, shape the future of the field and nurture young professionals.

Ed: This fella has his heart in the right place. If this is how you think and this is the path you're going to take, the world's gonna need you. Saddle up!

SHOULD I GO TO MEDICAL SCHOOL?

The mellow lifestyle of the Louisiana country doc

I have been practicing medicine for about six years now. I have a moderately successful practice in a rural town in southern Louisiana. I have a wife and 2 kids and a couple of ankle-biting frou-frou dogs, my wife's choice. I believe I have as much free time as any other successful professional that is devoted to his life's work — professionals other than physicians.

I exercise, attend social functions with pre-medicine friends and medical friends, participate in my kids' activities and lives, and am an avid recreational saltwater fisherman. I spend many weekends at my camp on the coast with family and friends. I am absolutely enjoying my life at this time and it was all made possible by becoming a physician.

Was med school tough? Hell yeah! But it was doable. I will be the first to admit that I will never be the doc to participate in cutting edge research or become the next guru in his respective field. However, I have staffed my clinic with great physicians that are more like that than I will ever be.

Personally, I am more than alright with that. I am able to treat patients and have a life. As far as financially, the early years are tough. Internships, residency and fellows are hell on the pocketbook but if you had any type of business sense the medical field is a very lucrative occupation. I work four days a week and off to the camp on Friday for the weekend. My kids are in private schools, we drive respectable vehicles, I have a camp and two boats, and live in a nice home. Everyone is entitled to their opinion but my life would be way different if not for becoming a physician.

SHOULD I GO TO MEDICAL SCHOOL?

The soldier turned pediatrician

There are the casualties of war in medicine for sure: Doctors who by sheer misfortune have a crap career. Doctors who mismanage their practices because of arrogance (think they are so smart that they know how to run a business with no business experience). Doctors who (when naïve young undergrads) have all the *wrong* reasons for entering the medical profession, such as: daddy/mommy, money, prestige, etc. Some people are just bitter, and will always have a negative outlook on life no matter what profession they are in. All polls and surveys are biased in a way by who actually responds to them.

I *hate* statistics that ask "if you had to do it again, would you?" It's a question for romantics and daydreamers. In reality, look where your feet are. If your head is somewhere else, of course you hate the present, you can't look around and enjoy it at all. You are always wanting something else out of life.

I was a 10 year military veteran before entering medical school, seeing deployments, hardships, and worse working hours than *any* medical resident (except maybe neurosurgeons, they are crazy). Medical school wasn't easy, especially the first two years. I had been out of the studying game for a while. The hardest part of the clinical years was dealing with residents or young attendings who had never experienced the real world, a decent salary, leadership, etc. I had to bite my tongue quite a bit, and when I didn't, my grade took a nice hit.

So I graduated and entered pediatrics. Quite a change from my prior military life indeed! Not a *single* person ever told me residency would be easy. If you want to do something easy, *don't* be a doctor. Go do something else, anything else.

I see doctors who hate people. I equally see a deeper-seated self-loathing and poor insight in general in those same doctors. I see doctors who sacrifice their health along the way, because they choose to. They choose to eat the crap hospital cafeteria food instead of the healthier options or pack a lunch. They choose to stop exercising. They choose to abandon all personal interests that contribute to their livelihood. They choose to keep making excuses how the medical world is against them, and they are just a victim.

I'm close to 40. I eat healthy, have a wonderful son, great friends, am in outstanding physical shape, volunteer, surf, read, study, coach, and do whatever the hell I want. The best part is, I get to do what I love everyday *and* get paid for it.

It should come as no shock that medical school is expensive. Luckily for me, I had the GI Bill to help pave my way through. The only reason I continued my application process is because I had reasonable expectations of being able to minimize my debt and was granted an opportunity to afford medical school through a decade of military service.

To the young and naïve: Going into debt at all costs for a dream is a huge price to pay, and you better be ready to pay it. You should accept that you dreamed of becoming a doctor, not becoming rich.

In the end, this is a great article for stimulation. I've been at this game for a long time, and it keeps getting better. It's a matter of perspective. If you are fed up with medical school, medicine or whatever, then change your perspective because

SHOULD I GO TO MEDICAL SCHOOL?

the world isn't going to change no matter where you go, what you do, or who you know.

Ed: Once again, a career in medicine turns out to be better than being shot at. And the GI Bill apparently makes a big difference — not an option most of us have access to.

5. ON LIFESTYLE & RELATIONSHIPS

SHOULD I GO TO MEDICAL SCHOOL?

My doctor wife makes more than I ever will

I'm an engineer in a relationship with a doc. Let me tell you, I was pretty ignorant of what doctors make. It's usually described as a "comfortable living." I only recently discovered that here, "comfortable" equates to a starting salary of around $140,000. Which is, y'know, a lot. More than the vast majority – myself included – can ever hope to attain in their lives.

So let me add another stress that wasn't expressed in the relationship section, and this one applies only to women: in addition to losing your prime years, you're also going to come out the gate out-earning essentially any guy who crosses your path, barring other doctors. While I'd like to pretend that I'm above such pettiness, I am forced to admit that it's tough as a man to accept that your partner is worth twice as much per hour to society as you are. I frankly doubt that I'll be able to keep this bitter pill down.

Ed: Probably the wrong time to tell the husband that his wife is underpaid.

SHOULD I GO TO MEDICAL SCHOOL?

Relationship challenges for women

I have no intention of being a dick with what I'm about to say. I'm just trying to relate some truth, from the distinct vantage point of my own noggin. It might be infuriating, but as a dude with sisters, i am sympathetic to the female condition, so I feel like I have to get this out there. Pardon the anonymity, but frankly, I feel like the following could get my lynched.

So I broke up with the doc I was dating. We're both 30 now. She has a few years before "advanced maternal age" sets in. And she's not as hot as she was in her twenties. There's no getting around the fact that this limits the pool of guys who see her as serious relationship material. Worse still, it seems like women don't like dating younger men, or men who earn less, so the pool of men *she* sees as serious relationship material is also greatly diminished.

Somehow this ex and I have managed to keep in touch without acrimony. She's been single since the breakup. She actually got a cat, and told me in so many words that it was because she was lonely. I feel for her. I thought I was gonna be in that situation – single at 30 – but things have actually gone in a different direction for me.

Since breaking up, I got a promotion, and I now have a low six-figure salary. It's not doctor money, but I'm debt free, and it's more than sufficient. I work a stress-free 40-hour week with tons of flexibility. This leaves me with plenty of cash and time to chase girls – and man, it's like shooting fish in a barrel. I'm having more success with 20-year old coeds than I did when i was 20! apparently, now that I'm educated,

SHOULD I GO TO MEDICAL SCHOOL?

traveled, and in a promising career, I'm more attractive than when i sat around smoking pot and playing Halo all day.

With the benefit of distance, I can see that while I was a little miffed at being out-earned by my ex, what really did us in was that I noticed my stock was rising in the dating market, and I couldn't resist the temptation. Yeah, it's true that some of these girls aren't very accomplished. But I've come to realize that professional accomplishment has *nothing at all* to do with relationship satisfaction. On top of that, I know I want a lot of kids one day (5, specifically) and, well, bottom line, it's easier to make healthy babies with a girl in her twenties than in her thirties.

Here's the real kicker: all of my ex's female colleagues are in a similar boat. Not a one is in a successful marriage or serious relationship, and several are divorced. Meanwhile, all of my friends ("bros", yeah, I'll cop to that) who failed to get married by 30 are having this startling realization: our dating lives are actually majorly improved over what they used to be.

The moral of the story is that medicine, as a career choice, may be disproportionately damaging to the romantic prospects for women. As Ali pointed out, medical training destroys relationships. So basically, any woman who aspires to medicine has an outsized chance of being a single thirty-something. And that's a much worse spot for women than for men (it's actually, at least by my anecdotal experience, a pretty chill spot for guys).

I've proofed this comment like five times now. I still expect a digital lynch mob, but keep in mind that i'm just trying to say something that I think young women should hear, because nobody else is gonna say it. Ultimately, it just corroborates

SHOULD I GO TO MEDICAL SCHOOL?

Ali's main point: don't do medicine unless you *can't imagine not doing it*. Otherwise, it just ain't worth it.

Ed: Like careers, relationships require time and effort. If all of your time and effort is going into a career, that leaves less for relationships. I wrote a whole book about this for women you may want to check out some time, called The Tao of Dating: The Smart Woman's Guide to Being Absolutely Irresistible.

SHOULD I GO TO MEDICAL SCHOOL?

The son of the absent doc speaks

As the son of a doctor, I can tell anyone reading this that choosing medicine as a profession can wreck a family. I hope I am unique in the fact that I hardly know my father. As a child growing up when my dad was in residency, I remember my father never being home, and asking my mom, "Where's daddy?", the answer always being "work." I eventually stopped asking and stopped wondering, and just accepted that I would never see him.

When I finally did see him, he was too stressed from work and detached from the family, and would often go straight to bed after coming home, even if it was 6:00 pm. Years passed, and here I am, 20, my father 52 and the routine persists–a 70 to 80 hour work week and no time for family. It's a horrible thing to say, but as the detached workaholic that he is, he has become more money-making machine than anything else to our family. Us kids and my mom reap the benefits, the house, the cars.

Hell, we kids actually get to live and love in the house; he only gets to sleep and drink in it. Think about it: you have to be so selfless to pursue medicine that you have to accept that your six figs are enjoyed primarily by your family (that you don't even know well), and not you. Is the fancy schmancy MD worth it? As per the only conversation I had with my dad this entire week, "No. If you want to go into medicine, be a PA. Or an NP. Hell, even a chiroquacktor. Anything but an MD."

SHOULD I GO TO MEDICAL SCHOOL?

The resident's husband 1 & 2

I'm married to a resident and this article is a very accurate portrayal of a resident's life. Her work schedule is insane. It's not just the amount of hours but the fact that these hours are packed and spent with difficult people and life or death situations. After a day of work she often mentions she didn't have time to eat or pee during the day. She has had some call shifts that lasted 40hrs straight (more than 3 days) where she got only 3 to 4 hours sleep breaks per night plus a few eating breaks here and there because it was busy the whole time. That meant no time for a shower in those three days, only superficial cleanups and quick change of scrubs when things got too bloody/amniotic.

***

Married to a final year surgery resident and unfortunately this article rings very true. I'm not sure if the profession changed at some point, but if we were advising my kid now on future professions, doctor would not be on that list. I remember the idealism that my wife went into the profession with and that is completely gone now. I find that very sad.

6. THE 360° VIEW FROM PRACTITIONERS

SHOULD I GO TO MEDICAL SCHOOL?

Interview with Dean Ornish, M.D.

AB: So here's the idea: medicine used to be this prestigious, fulfilling, well-compensated profession and things have shifted significantly in the last few years, which is why I wrote the "Why You Should Not Go to Med School" article. I was the only person in my class to not to do residency, which was considered heresy at the time. Now it has become much more common. But people still struggle with this. There are a lot of people who are applying every year and they're wondering, "What should I do?"

What prompted the interview with you was that I bumped into the daughter of my dean from UCSD Medical School, and she said "By the way don't tell anyone, but my mom forbid me from going to medical school." So I thought it was very telling that the dean of my medical school would not let her own kids go into medicine.

DO: Why? For all the reasons you outlined?

AB: Partially, but if the dean is saying this to her own daughter, that's very telling about the whole profession. So I thought it would be useful to ask actual physicians who are practicing and have children of their own, what do you think? If you had a kid right now that said, "Dad I want to go to med school," what would you say?

DO: I would say "Great!" because I think that med school is a really good idea. Now, it depends on what you want to do with it. If you just want to practice traditional medicine — particularly primary care medicine - I think that can be challenging. I get that a lot of doctors — most doctors, according to surveys, wouldn't recommend medicine for their sons or daughters. The dean of UCSD is just part of a much larger trend.

And many doctors would leave the profession if they could just because it's not fun if you're practicing the kind of medicine that is currently being practiced where you have to see a new patient every eight minutes. You don't really have time to talk about the things that really matter, in terms of what they're eating, how they're responding to stress, what's going on in their marriage and their school and their work and their home. You basically just have time to listen to their heart and lungs, write a prescription for something, and you're off to the next patient. It's profoundly unsatisfying for both doctors and patients.

AB: Profoundly unsatisfying.

DO: Yeah. For both doctors and patients. I think that's one of the reasons why more money was spent out of pocket for alternative medicine than traditional medicine the last 10 or 15 years because those practitioners spend time with you. They don't interrupt you, they touch you, they listen to you, they do all the things that people really want to make them feel seen, heard, and validated.

So now some people would say that is only going to get worse because the Affordable Care Act and Obamacare kick in and doctors are making even less money, working even harder for less money, and there are even more reasons not to go to medical school.

But I think a different perspective, which is personal for me, is that medicine is more of a calling than a job. There are lots of easier ways to make money, so if your goal is to make money quickly, then medicine is not the way to do it. In fact, if you believe people like Peter Thiel, *college* is not the way to do it. Just get a job and do something.

But life is a lot more to me than just making money. It's about *meaning*. And to do work that is meaningful is really important to me. It's like the old adage: "Do what you love and then you don't feel like you're working." And so if your goal is to have a prestigious job that makes you lots of money, there are lots of easier ways to do that.

If you feel like you're kind of called to service and that brings meaning and joy in your life, on the other hand — I mean to me, for example, being able to save someone's life is really meaningful. I was just having breakfast at a hotel in Los Angeles last month and someone had a cardiac arrest at the next table and I was able to revive them. That's fun. That's nice to be able to do. I don't like that feeling of feeling helpless. Whether or not I ever practice medicine it's nice to have those skills because they stay with you.

In the same way, medicine has such flexibility that you can do anything with it. There are a thousand things that you can do that are already out there, and you can create your own path as I've done because it gives you the flexibility to do that. So I like what I've been able to do in my career and medicine gives kind of a grounding and a credibility that I wouldn't have otherwise had.

There are so many good ideas out there. My brother is fond of saying, "Keep an open mind but not so open that your brains fall out," and so medicine gives you kind of a grounding. It's only one perspective but it's a *useful* perspective and it's one that you can build on and branch out from as I've done.

SHOULD I GO TO MEDICAL SCHOOL?

So I like that part of it. And it's nice to be able to make a living pretty much anywhere in the world and certainly anywhere in the U.S., so I like the freedom that that affords. And people can always go into concierge medicine if they want to have less hassles and more money and not deal with insurance companies and spend more time with patients. So those models are evolving fairly quickly as alternatives to the traditional fee-for-service kind of medicine.

But the main reason that I like it, the real issue for me, is the meaning that it provides. The real epidemic in our culture is that sense of loneliness and isolation and lack of meaning that what you do really makes a difference. And if you're in a corporate world you spend so much time dealing with the politics of things rather than what's really the right thing to do. There are exceptions to that, but that's the norm.

So if my kids said they wanted to go to medical school I'd say, great — just don't have any illusions. I mean, yeah, it takes a lot of time. People say, "Oh it's so many years and you work so hard." Well yeah, but you're going to spend those years anyway. I mean if you spend seven years — four years in medical school and three years of residency — it's not like you're in solitary confinement somewhere. You're going to be spending those seven years doing something.

So it sort of just becomes a question of not "How long does it take?" but "Are you enjoying that along the way?" Even things like internships and residencies are not nearly as bad as they were when I was going through it, where you're on call every second or third night, because they have laws now that you can only work a certain amount of hours. And if you're doing a startup people are working 100-110 hours a week.

SHOULD I GO TO MEDICAL SCHOOL?

If you're doing anything that is really meaningful, the fact that it's hard is part of what *makes* it meaningful. Otherwise it's like "big deal." I mean I get bored easily anyways. I like things that are challenges. It took me 16 years to get Medicare to cover my program. That's ridiculous. But it made it really meaningful. When my wife had our kids it's really hard going through labor and nine months kind of with this thing you're carrying around with you, but that's part of what makes it meaningful.

So I'd be really thrilled if they wanted to go into medicine. I'm not pushing them, I'm not forbidding them. I'm saying "I'll support whatever works for you."

AB: The call of service is really one of the reasons why people get into medicine and want to do it and you mentioned that. And what happens is that people end up on this conveyor belt, and they get into medical school and they're doing their thing, and now they're in a whole bunch of debt. If they think, "Oh, I'm going to go into preventive medicine," well that's not going to pay the bills, so that's why they get shunted into some other higher-paying specialty.

What would you say to somebody who is really into the whole idea of medicine as service? The whole idea of really being able to sit down and be a healer and have time — not the eight-minute appointment.

DO: Well that's the model that we're creating. We got Medicare to cover my program. They'll pay for 72 hours of training which would divide into 18 four-hour sessions. The physician is quarterback and works with a nurse, a dietitian, a yoga teacher, an exercise physiologist, and a clinical psychologist. So the patients come for four-hour sessions. They get an hour of yoga and meditation, an hour of support group which is really an intentional community, an hour of supervised exercise, and then an hour of a group meal with a lecture.

And the doctor is really more like a quarterback and doesn't have to spend a huge amount of time doing that, so that frees him or her up to do other stuff. But they're providing these types of services and because Medicare and other insurance companies are now paying for it, it allows them to make a very comfortable living practicing the kind of medicine that they want to be doing.

And I think that the good thing about Obamacare is that it's changing the incentives away from fee-for-service procedures — like the more stents you put in and the more angioplasties you do the more money you make — to "here is X amount of dollars to take care of somebody" and whatever you don't spend on them you get to keep. So it completely turns the incentives on their ear and says the kinds of things that we're doing are now financially viable and sustainable for people.

So we're trying to really create a new paradigm of medicine that is not only more caring and more compassionate but also more cost-effective and competent by addressing the more fundamental causes of why people get sick, which will largely be the lifestyle choices that we're making each day. So that's really meaningful and fun.

In my work, because I am often fundraising for my research and for various other reasons, I've had the good fortune to spend a lot of time getting to know some very powerful, successful, household-name people. And those clichés are really true that once you have a certain amount of money — like $75,000 a year is what some studies show — more money and more power don't really bring you more happiness.

SHOULD I GO TO MEDICAL SCHOOL?

And certainly you can make that threshold as a doctor without too much trouble and that what really matters is the things that are harder to quantify. And so you find people like Paul Farmer out there who are very, very happy people not making a lot of money who are doing amazing good in the world and it's incredibly meaningful. It's hard to do that in other professions to the same degree where you're really touching people and when they're coming to you in their most vulnerable time. The level on intimacy that you can connect with people is really deep which is also makes it meaningful.

So for all of those reasons — of course it's hard and it takes time, but you could also structure a lifestyle — it doesn't mean that you have to go into dermatology if you don't want to. Just make less money, see fewer patients. Or if you want to partner with a group and say, like a Kaiser Permanente, "I'm only going to work these certain hours," then you can do that.

A lot of doctors are getting bought by hospitals so that they deal with all the infrastructure in the building and all that and they can focus more on what they want to do. Or they go into concierge medicine as I mentioned. So there are so many ways of structuring a lifestyle that can grow with your own values but it still provides you the opportunity to make a meaningful difference in the lives of people that, to me, make all the challenges worth it. I know that's not exactly supporting the thesis of your book but...

AB: Actually, you're saying the same stuff but you're just framing it more positively, like "This is why you *should* become a doctor."

SHOULD I GO TO MEDICAL SCHOOL?

DO: Not why you should but why, if those things are not deterrents to you, why it's worth it. To me it is. The fact that it's hard, it takes a lot of time, that is appealing to a lot of people. The Marines are looking for a few good men — whatever. I think that — I don't know if you go to the regular TED conferences but there was a TED Talk a few years ago and I can't remember if it was Wade from National Geographic or whoever it was. The explorer.

AB: Wade Davis?

DO: Wade Davis. Yeah. Thank you. But it was talking about a mission to Antarctica and it was like "low wages, good chance you're going to die on the trip, and freezing cold" and they got more applications than they could handle.

AB: Right. Well there is the old Shackleton ad.

DO: I think that's the one.

AB: Oh. Oh I see.

DO: The Shackleton ad?

AB: It's the Shackleton ad. Yeah.

DO: What is that?

AB: The Shackleton ad says - it's really short. It says "difficult journey, unknown place, very cold, bad food, possibility of death, chance for glory."

DO: Yeah. That's the one. And they had more applicants than they could deal with.

AB: Right.

SHOULD I GO TO MEDICAL SCHOOL?

DO: So the idea that it's hard doesn't necessarily mean that it's bad, that's going to be part of the fun.

AB: But these people who responded they were really into the idea and they were into it for the right reason which is that, "We're going to go on an adventure, it's going to be hard, and whatever happens we're cool with it."

DO: Right.

AB: I think a lot of kids are going to med school thinking, "Oh here is the plush little ride I'm going to go on, I'm going to have my cushy little office" and then they're hit by it. So what I'd like to ask you about is the idea of the calling. And that is one of the big things I tell people that this is not some kind of job to make mom happy, something that will pay the bills, or something you should do because you think it's a prestigious job, or any of these things. It has to be something that comes from the heart of you. You want to treat sick people. You want to make people feel better. And I say the one question you have to ask is, "Would I be happier doing anything but treating sick people?"

DO: Well it's not necessarily treating sick people. I spend a lot of time doing health policy, getting Medicare coverage changed in the reimbursement system, dealing with creating a whole new paradigm of medical care, of health care not just sick care, of lecturing at TEDx or TED or wherever, of empowering people with information. It's really fun and it takes me to a lot of places, like this, that I would never have done before. So I think it's important to on the one hand give a reality check and say, hey, this is hard, but to not neglect the other half of that.

It's not just for people who have a calling who want to be Mother Teresa or Albert Schweitzer and take care of sick people and make them feel better. That's a small part of medicine. The nice thing about medicine is it gives you access to so many opportunities and platforms — ones that are currently there but also ones that you can create your own path and so something that no one has ever done before, not to mention all the research opportunities and things that we've been doing and writing books and things like that you can do that you wouldn't otherwise be able to do. So we're limited only by our imaginations.

I think it's really a useful service to make sure that people understand that it's not Mary Poppins but at the same time that it's not a lump of coal either. There are so many things that you can do that maybe aren't even out there yet, that it gives you that kind of freedom. It's good that people go in with their eyes open but at the same time you don't want to turn people off who don't understand that there are a lot of good things in there beyond the challenges.

We've outlined the challenges and the dark side very well and I think that's useful but I think not only from a standpoint of balance and fairness but just from the standpoint of not wanting to turn off somebody who might otherwise really enjoy this because there is a whole different side to it that most people don't know about.

AB: So I like the idea of here is this one question you can ask yourself and if the answer is "yes" then go, if the answer is "no" then don't go. So if you were to formulate that question for a 19 year old who is doing their premed requirements, what would that be?

DO: Well, see I wouldn't frame it like that because I don't think it's quite like that. I mean if you say "Is medicine your calling?," well that's kind of simplistic. But it's more like here are the advantages, here are the challenges. It is really hard, it is going to take a lot of your time depending on what specialty you go in, you don't really make much money while you're being trained, but you're also learning an incredible amount.

So you have to decide if it's worth it to you. You lose a lot of freedom during your training but then you get a huge amount of freedom when you're done because you can live anywhere, you can practice in a million different ways, you can create your own path as we've talked about. So I don't think that you can reduce that down to an algorithm of one question. I think it's really so much more complicated than that.

I think it's really important that people go into that with their eyes open but at the same time eyes open to all possibilities not just to the dark side of it. Most people don't go into medicine thinking it's an easy path.

There has certainly been enough TV shows and books and movies about it such that most people know that it's hard. And they hear a lot of doctors grumbling about how the Golden Age of medicine has passed and "I wouldn't let me kid go into it" and "I'd get out of it if I could" and all those kinds of things. But they also need to hear that I am so happy to be a doctor. I would highly recommend it for my kids as long as they understood all the different aspects of it.

AB: Right. Well I think you've taken the initiative to carve out the niche that works for you. For a lot of people they feel more — they feel like they're subject to these various waves that they don't really control.

DO: But it's true about anything you go into. Let's say you wanted to do a tech thing. Well you can go work as a grunt and eat pizza all night and get paid not necessarily all that much. Or you could take the initiative and do what Bill Gates or Steve Jobs or other people have done.

It's the same personality characteristics of empowering yourself and taking charge of your life and not being limited by what other people's views or constraints or customs are that you're willing to say, "Hey I don't mind failing, even if I fail I'm going to learn something." I mean when I work with people who are on their deathbeds they don't regret what they've done; they usually regret what they didn't do.

Because even if you do something and you fail you learned something from it. That's a very valuable lesson even if it was a "failure" and then it comes out of your own experience. So it's not like you're borrowing someone else's wisdom; it's really coming out of your own life experiences. I think that's great.

So that's why I think that nobody has a monopoly on truth. And the more perspectives that I can see the world through, it's like more pixels in a picture, or like the parable of the blind men and the elephant, more parts of the elephant. And medicine is a very powerful and a very limited way of looking at the world and as long as you recognize that it's limited then you can appreciate the power of it.

And then you can bring in other perspectives as I've tried to do, and continue to do that, which make me that much more effective even within the realm of being a doctor, *especially* in the realm of being a doctor. And that makes it so much more fun and interesting. If your idea of medicine is you're going to go and see a new patient every eight minutes and be looking in ears and prescribing pills, and you never really have time to talk about things that really matter, and you never really have time even to connect with your patients, that's not fun. But it doesn't have to be that way.

AB: I think a big part of it is just having your heart in the right place and for the right reasons. Lest you think I am anti-medicine, the world needs doctors, but I think it needs the right doctors.

DO: I think it's great to the extent that you weed out people who are going into it just because they think it's going to be a good way to get rich, but I don't think most people think that anymore.

AB: And I don't think it's necessarily an easy way to get rich.

DO: No, it's a very hard way to get rich.

AB: It's a long way to go. Thanks so much for your time, Dr Ornish. This has been a very enlightening conversation.

SHOULD I GO TO MEDICAL SCHOOL?

Interview with Ashvin Pande, M.D., Interventional Radiologist

AB: How did you decide to go to medical school?

AP: When I first came to college, I was thinking about it. I ultimately decided not to. I said I was not going to follow the lemmings to medical school. I was a physics major, and then I was interested in some other things, and felt a bit lost.

I got into an automobile accident my sophomore year. I was jogging on the BU Bridge and got hit by a car. It was completely my fault – I ran into the street, I wasn't looking, I got hit by a van. The next thing I know, I was waking up at the Beth Israel Hospital. Ultimately, I had a broken collarbone, a concussion and a facial laceration that required repair, but I was lucky to be alive.

I remember waking up. I was terrified and started crying. I had a lot of thoughts going on in my mind, but one of them was that I didn't want to die, and I wanted to be a doctor. There were people who said, "Look, you're going to be fine." They sutured up my face. And I thought, "Wow. If you could be someone who can provide that kind of comfort, that kind of service to someone else, that would be pretty meaningful." To have that gift, or power, or whatever you want to call it. It's meaningful.

Most of us walk through life, and we can offer people our company. But to actually make people feel better… So at that point I said to myself, "You know what? I'm going to go to medical school." It was my junior year, and I had already done enough physics and science classes to fulfill the prerequisites so it all worked out.

SHOULD I GO TO MEDICAL SCHOOL?

I went through medical school; it was hard work but I enjoyed it. I went through residency, and in spite of the stresses of it and the burnout, it was incredibly gratifying. The first year of fellowship I felt was the hardest of my training but also the most gratifying, because I felt I was useful. Before that, I wasn't all that useful, but the more you train, the more useful you get.

From that point until where I am now, I've had some frustrations, and I've sort of gone up and down. Your question is one that I think about a lot. You know, I did a long segment of training, I did some research which did not turn out very well. I felt like I wasted several years in that.

I did two additional years of interventional radiology training. Interventional radiology is fun, but I've been doing it for 7-8 years now, there's a lot of night call. You're up a lot. And there's a lot of frustration in medicine with the bureaucratic nature of it, too. I feel like that with all the documentation, electronic medical records, and regulatory environment, if you're not in the operating room doing surgery, you're basically a glorified data entry person.

Because it used to be when we rounded, we walked around and we'd see the patients. Rounding now is now six people around six computers typing stuff in. You should come see any modern teaching hospital. Rounding now is that we sit in a pod, an attending, a fellow, and three residents. We each have a computer in front of us, typing stuff in; maybe the resident has two windows open, one for notes and one for billing. You say, "Okay, let's go see the patient." The patient was admitted by the night float. Nobody has actually seen the patient. You're reading a note that someone else has written.

SHOULD I GO TO MEDICAL SCHOOL?

You go see the patient for maybe five minutes, then you come out and say, "Okay, what are we going to do?", you type it all in, then you go to the next one.

The only reprieve I have from that is that I actually do procedures. So I feel like I'm still doing something. It's a deeply cynical view, but it's one that reflects the frustration that a lot of doctors have with modern medicine. When I see that, I wonder: if you're training in that environment, as an intern or a med student, it's essentially learning electronic medical records (EMR), entering data, cutting and pasting, making sure you have everything.

What people have failed to understand is that the documentation is actually obscuring the transmission of information. If I review notes now, I have to go through six pages of notes before finding the nugget of information I'm actually looking for. And then I'm not sure whether this was just copied and pasted from three weeks ago, or is this what happened today.

And I've wondered in the past year, "Is this what I want to keep doing?" I will say, the work when you get to the core of medicine is supposed to be about (for me in this case) doing major procedures like heart valve replacements, heart attacks. That's meaningful in a way that few of my friends who are in finance or law can probably approach. When patients come back to you and they say, boy I feel much better than I did before – that's powerful.

And we talked about saving lives, and that's a bit melodramatic, and I'm certainly not saving lives every day, but you are trying to make people better in a way they weren't before – "I can do this that I couldn't do before." That's meaningful. People who are in their middle age, we start to look for meaning in life. And if I ever left medicine, I'd be hard-pressed to find that ever again.

For me I see one case at a time, I see one patient at a time – it's micro. If I were to do something else, I would think about what I can do that's macro, that has bigger impact. When I see young people interested in medicine, I just don't know what it's going to look like.

If I were presented with the vision of a person in the office all day, sitting in front of the computer, seeing patients for 10 minutes and then documenting for maybe 15 minutes, I would find it potentially ungratifying. Because at worst, you're just doing data entry. And there's a limited amount of time. The more time you're spending on data entry and checking off meaningful use and meeting regulatory and billing requirements, the less you're actually practicing medicine. I think that's something that medicine will have to face. EMR in its current incarnation, if not a cancer eating up our time, is at best a clumsy Version 1.0 of what it should be. It cannot last in its current form because it's destructive of medicine.

AB: If you were to go back in time as a pre-med, what would you wish you knew that you know now?

AP: I'm not sure I would do anything differently. I feel like the choices I made were honest and genuine, and not done for any insincere reason. I would have focused my medicine career a bit more. I feel like the time I spent doing molecular biology research was probably not done for the right reasons but rather because I felt it was what was expected.

SHOULD I GO TO MEDICAL SCHOOL?

I've always had some interest in business and entrepreneurship. I still would have done medicine, but I feel like a lot of the dynamism of medicine is there. If there's anything I miss in medicine – well, it's a long training program and you've got to walk the straight and narrow, and I wish there were more creativity in it, the opportunity to do things outside the box. I continuously search for ways to do that. I like the idea of how you can change the economics or incentives in medicine to make it better. At the same time, I have no reason to believe that if I had done it over again, I would be anywhere different right now.

AB: How did you pick your specialty?

AP: In medical school, I liked procedural work. I liked surgery. I didn't like the personality of surgery. I felt it was a bit toxic and angry, and didn't fit me in a way that I liked. But I liked the idea of performing surgery. I also liked the cognitive aspect of medicine. So I asked myself what's the closest between the two, where I can do something like surgery but I don't have to train in surgery. Interventional cardiology fit that bill as well as anything. And now, a lot of the procedures that we do overlap with cardiac surgery. I do heart valve replacements. I actually partner with a cardiac surgeon and we do it together.

AB: If your kids wanted to go into medicine, what would you tell them?

AP: Make sure you're going into it for the right reasons. If you're going into it because it's a comfortable living, or prestigious, it may be that you're not making as much money as you think you will be. And this is probably no different from any of the advice any of us got for anything, but if you feel like you're doing it because the work that you're doing is meaningful, then that's the right reason.

Like I said, my concerns about the structural changes of medical practice remain. I don't know if the digitalization of medical record-keeping is going to improve or progress in a way that's going to make medicine completely unappealing. I wouldn't necessarily discourage my kids from going in as long as they're doing it for the right reasons.

As far as interventional cardiology goes, I would say yes, but with caution. As far as night call goes, it's one of the worst. And as I get older, frankly I look forward to not being woken up at 2am every other night to do cases. So I would say you have to be careful about that.

I would say that this specialty has evolved a lot, especially in the past ten years. It's a young specialty, and I'd just be cautious going into it. I think it's gratifying when you're doing it, but be cautious getting into it, because to be honest with you, it's different than even when I started it. Because angioplasties have fallen in volume and some procedures fallen out of favor, but we've found other things to do. But if that changes and you don't find other things to do, the field could shrink. You just don't know.

AB: If you could do it all over again, would you choose medicine as a career?

AP: Yes. You know, my brother's in banking and private equity, and look, am I jealous every once in a while about how much money he's making? I'm not insensitive to the needs of money, or how nice it would be to have a house in Nantucket or the Hamptons. But would I want to wake up every morning and be a bond trader, even if I were making $5m a year? The answer to that is definitely no. The thing is, even when this work sucks, when you can do something great for somebody, that's powerful. Every day we're alive, we're essentially filling our obituaries. What do you want written on there? What are we doing that makes our lives meaningful?

Another example that's relevant to this question would be my wife, who trained at Harvard for med school, residency and fellowship. Now she's working at a medical behavioral change startup. It's very unlikely that she'll go back to clinical practice, because it's such exciting and interesting work at her startup. But if you were to ask her, she'd say that she'd still do it all over again, because that's what got her to where she is right now.

7. ALTERNATIVE CAREER PATHS

SHOULD I GO TO MEDICAL SCHOOL?

Why You Should Become a Nurse or Physician's Assistant Instead of a Doctor: The Underrated Perils of Medical School, by Jake Seliger

Many if not most people who go to medical school are making a huge mistake—one they won't realize they've made until it's too late to undo.

So many medical students, residents, and doctors say they wish they could go back in time and tell themselves to do something—anything—else. Their stories are so similar that they've inspired me to explain, in detail, the underappreciated yet essential problems with medical school and residency. Potential doctors also don't realize becoming a nurse or physicians assistant (PA) provides many of the job security advantages of medical school without binding those who start to at least a decade, and probably a lifetime, of finance-induced servitude.

The big reasons to be a doctor are a) *lifetime* earning potential, b) the limited number of doctors who are credentialed annually, which implies that doctors can restrict supply and thus will always have jobs available, c) higher perceived social status, and d) a desire to "help people" (there will be much more on the dubious value of that last one below).

These reasons come with numerous problems: a) it takes a long time for doctors to make that money, b) it's almost impossible to gauge whether you'll actually like a profession or the process of joining that profession until you're already done, c) most people underestimate opportunity costs, and d) you have to be able to help yourself before you can help other people (and the culture of medicine and medical education is toxic).

Straight talk about doctors and money.

You're reading this because you tell your friends and maybe yourself that you "want to help people," but let's start with the cash. Although many doctors will eventually make a lot of money, they take a *long* time to get there. Nurses can start making real salaries of around $50,000 when they're 22. Doctors can't start making real money until they're at least 29, and often not until they're much older.

Keep that in mind when you read the following numbers.

Student Doctor reports that family docs make about $130 – $200K on average, which sounds high compared to what I've heard on the street (Student Doctor's numbers also don't discuss hours worked). The Bureau of Labor Statistics—a more reliable source—reports that primary care physicians make an *average* of $186,044 per year. Notice, however, that's an average, and it also doesn't take into account overhead. Notice too that the table showing that BLS data indicates more than 40% of doctors are in primary care specialties. Family and general practice doctors make a career median annual wage of $163,510.

Nurses, by contrast, make about $70K a year. They also have a lot of market power—especially skilled nurses who might otherwise be doctors. Christine Mackey-Ross describes these economic dynamics in "The New Face of Health Care: Why Nurses Are in Such High Demand." Nurses are gaining market power because medical costs are rising and residency programs have a stranglehold on the doctor supply. More providers must come from *somewhere*. As we know from Econ 101, when you limit supply in the face of rising demand, prices rise.

The limit on the number of doctors is pretty sweet if you're *already* a doctor, because it means you have very little competition and, if you choose a sufficiently demanding specialty, you can make a lot of money. But it's bad for the healthcare system as a whole because too many patients chase too few doctors. Consequently, the system is lurching in the direction of finding ways to provide healthcare at lower costs. Like, say, through nurses and PAs.

Those nurses and PAs are going to end up competing with primary care docs. Look at one example, from the *New York Times's* "U.S. Moves to Cut Back Regulations on Hospitals:"

Under the proposals, issued with a view to "impending physician shortages," it would be easier for hospitals to use "advanced practice nurse practitioners and physician assistants in lieu of higher-paid physicians." This change alone "could provide immediate savings to hospitals," the administration said.

Primary care docs are increasingly going to see pressure on their wages from nurse practitioners for as long as health care costs outstrip inflation. Consider "Yes, the P.A. Will See You Now:"

Ever since he was a hospital volunteer in high school, Adam Kelly was interested in a medical career. What he wasn't interested in was the lifestyle attached to the M.D. degree. "I wanted to treat patients, but I wanted free time for myself, too," he said. "I didn't want to be 30 or 35 before I got on my feet — and then still have a lot of loans to pay back."

SHOULD I GO TO MEDICAL SCHOOL?

To recap: nurses start making money when they're 22, not 29, *and* they are eating into the market for primary care docs. Quality of care is a concern, but the evidence thus far shows no difference between nurse practitioners who act as primary-care providers and MDs who do.

Calls to lower doctor pay, like the one found in Matt Yglesias's "We pay our doctors way too much," are likely to grow louder. Note that I'm not taking a moral or economic stance on whether physician pay **should** be higher or lower: I'm arguing that the pressure on doctors' pay is likely to increase because of fundamental forces on healthcare.

To belabor the point about money, *The Atlantic* recently published "The average female primary-care physician would have been financially better off becoming a physician assistant." Notice: "Interestingly, while the PA field started out all-male, the majority of graduates today are female. The PA training program is generally 2 years, shorter than that for doctors. Unsurprisingly, subsequent hourly earnings of PAs are lower than subsequent hourly earnings of doctors."

Although the following sentence doesn't use the word "opportunity costs," it should: "Even though both male and female doctors both earn higher wages than their PA counterparts, most female doctors don't work enough hours at those wages to financially justify the costs of becoming a doctor." I'm not arguing that women shouldn't become doctors. But I am arguing that women *and* men both underestimate the opportunity costs of med school. If they understood those costs, fewer would go.

Plus, if you get a nursing degree, *you can still go to medical school* (as long as you have the pre-requisite courses; hell, you can major in English and go to med school as long as you take the biology, math, physics, and chemistry courses that med schools require). Apparently some medical schools will sniff at nurses who want to become doctors because of the nursing shortage and, I suspect, because med schools want to maintain a clear class / status hierarchy with doctors at top. Med schools are run by doctors invested in the doctor mystique. But the reality is simpler: medical schools want people with good MCAT scores and GPAs. Got a 4.0 and whatever a high MCAT score is? A med school will defect and take you.

One medical resident friend read a draft of this essay and simply said that she "didn't realize that I was looking for nursing." Or being PA. She hated her third year of medical school, as most med students do, and got shafted in her residency—which she effectively can't leave. Adam Kelly is right: more people should realize what "the lifestyle attached to an M.D. degree" means.

They should also understand "The Bullying Culture of Medical School" and residency, which is pervasive and pernicious—and it contributes to the relationship failures that notoriously plague the medical world. Yet med schools and residencies can get away with this because they have you by the loans.

Why *would* my friend have realized that she wanted to be a nurse? Our culture doesn't glorify nursing the way it does doctoring (except, maybe, on Halloween and in adult cinema). High academic achievers think being a doctor is the optimal road to success in the medical world. They see eye-popping surgeon salary numbers and rhetoric about helping people without realizing that nurses help people too, or that their desire to help people is likely to be pounded out of them by a cold, uncaring system that uses the rhetoric of helping to sucker undergrads into mortgaging their souls to student loans. Through the magic of student loans, schools are steadily siphoning off more of doctors' lifetime earnings. Given constraints and barriers to entry into medicine, I suspect med schools and residencies will be able to continue doing so for the foreseeable future. The logical response for individuals is exit the market because they have so little control over it.

Sure, $160K/year probably sounds like a lot to a random 21-year-old college student, because it is, but after taking into account the investment value of money, student loans for undergrad, student loans for med school, how much nurses make, and residents' salaries, most doctors' earnings probably fail to outstrip nurses' earnings until well after the age of 40. Dollars per hour worked probably don't outstrip nurses' earnings until even later.

To some extent, you're trading happiness, security, dignity, and your sex life in your 20s, and possibly early 30s, for a financial opportunity that *might not pay off until your 50s.*

Social status is nice, but not nearly as nice when you're exhausted at 3 a.m. as a third-year, or exhausted at 3 a.m. as a first-year resident, or exhausted at 3 a.m. as a third-year resident and you're 30 and you just want a quasi-normal life, damnit, and maybe some time to be an artist. Or when you're exhausted at 3 a.m. as an attending on-call physician because the senior doctors at the HMO know how to stiff the newbies by forcing them to "pay their dues."

SHOULD I GO TO MEDICAL SCHOOL?

This is where prospective medical students protest, "I'm not going to be a family medicine doc." Which is okay: maybe you won't be. Have fun in five or seven years of residency instead of three. But don't confuse the salaries of superstar specialties like neurosurgery and cardiology with the average experience; more likely than not you're average. There's this social ideal of doctors being rich. Not all are, even with barriers to entry in place.

The underrated miseries of residency

As one resident friend said, "You can see why doctors turn into the kind of people they do." He meant that the system itself lets patients abuse doctors, doctors abuse residents, and for people to generally treat each other not like people, but like cogs. At least nurses who discover they hate nursing can quit, since they will have a portable undergrad degree and won't have obscene graduate school student loans. They can probably go back to school and get a second degree in twelve to twenty-four months. (Someone with a standard bachelor's degree can probably enter nursing in the same time period.)

In normal jobs, a worker who learns about a better opportunity in another company or industry can pursue it. Students sufficiently dissatisfied with their university can transfer.[1] Many academic grad schools make quitting easy. Residencies don't. The residency market is tightly controlled by residency programs that want to restrict residents' autonomy—and thus their wages and bargaining power. Once you're in a residency, it's very hard to leave, and you can only do so at particular in the gap between each residency year.

SHOULD I GO TO MEDICAL SCHOOL?

This is a recipe for exploitation; many of the labor battles during the first half of the twentieth century were fought to prevent employers from wielding this kind of power. For medical residents, however, employers have absolute power enshrined in law—though employers cloak their power in the specious word "education."

Once a residency program has you, they can do almost anything they want to you, and you have little leverage. You don't want to be in situations where you have no leverage, yet that's precisely what happens the moment you enter the "match."

Let's explain the match, since almost no potential med students understand it. The match occurs in the second half of the fourth year of medical school. Students apply to residencies in the first half of their fourth year, interview at potential hospitals, and then list the residencies they're interested in. Residency program directors then rank the students, and the National Residency Match Program "matches" students to programs using a hazily described algorithm.

Students are then obligated to attend that residency program. They can't privately negotiate with other programs, as students can for, say, undergrad admissions, or med school admissions—or almost any other normal employment situation. Let me repeat and bold: **Residents can't negotiate**. They can't say, "How about another five grand?" or "Can I modify my contract to give me fewer days?" If a resident refuses to accept her "match," then she's blackballed from re-entering for **the next three years**.

SHOULD I GO TO MEDICAL SCHOOL?

Residency programs have formed a cartel designed to control cost and reduce employee autonomy, and hence salaries. I only went to law school for a year, by accident, but even I know enough law and history to recognize a very clear situation of the sort that anti-trust laws are supposed to address in order to protect workers. When my friend entered the match process like a mouse into a snake's mouth, I became curious, because the system's cruelty, exploitation, and unfairness to residents is an obvious example of employers banding together to harm employees. Lawyers often get a bad rap—sometimes for good reasons—but the match looked ripe for lawyers to me.

It turns out that I'm not a legal genius and that real lawyers have noticed this anti-trust violation. An anti-trust lawsuit was filed in the early 2000s. Read about it in the *NYTimes*, including a grimly hilarious line about how "The defendants say the Match is intended to help students and performs a valuable service." Ha! A valuable service to *employers*, since employees effectively can't quit or negotiate with individual employers. Curtailing employee power by distorting markets is a valuable service. The article also noted regulatory capture:

> *Meanwhile, the medical establishment, growing increasingly concerned about the legal fees and the potential liability for hundreds of millions of dollars in damages, turned to Congress for help. They hired lobbyists to request legislation that would exempt the residency program from the accusations. A rider, sponsored by Senators Edward M. Kennedy, Democrat of Massachusetts, and Judd Gregg, Republican of New Hampshire, was attached to a pension act, which President Bush signed into law in April.*

In other words, **employers bought Congress and President Bush in order to screw residents.**[2] If you attend med school, you're agreeing to be screwed for three to eight years after you've incurred hundreds of thousands of dollars of debt, and you have few if any legal rights to attack the exploitative system you've entered.

(One question I have for knowledgeable readers: do you know of any comprehensive discussion of residents and unions? Residents can apparently unionize—which, if I were a medical resident, would be my first order of business—but the only extended treatment of the issue I've found so far is here, which deals with a single institution. Given how poorly residents are treated, I'm surprised there haven't been more unionization efforts, especially in union-friendly, resident-heavy states like California and New York. One reason might be simple: people fear being blackballed at their ultimate jobs, and a lot of residents seem to have Stockholm Syndrome.)

Self-interested residency program directors will no doubt argue that residency is set up the way it is because the residency experience is educational. So will doctors. Doctors argue for residency being essential because they have a stake in the process. Residency directors and other administrators make money off residents who work longer hours and don't have alternatives. We shouldn't be surprised that they seek other legal means of restricting competition—so much of the fight around medicine isn't about patient care; it's about regulatory environments and legislative initiatives. For one recent but very small example of the problems, see "When the Nurse Wants to Be Called 'Doctor'," concerning nursing doctorates.

I don't buy their arguments for more than ad hominem reasons. The education at many residency programs is tenuous at best. One friend, for example, is in a program that requires residents to attend "conference," where residents are supposed to learn. But "conference" usually degenerates into someone nattering and most of the residents reading or checking their phones. Conference is mandatory, regardless of its utility. Residents aren't 10 year olds, yet they're treated as such.

These problems are well-known ("What other profession routinely kicks out a third of its seasoned work force and replaces it with brand new interns every year?"). But there's no political impetus to act: doctors like limiting their competition, and people are still fighting to get into medical school.

Soldiers usually make four-year commitments to the military. Even ROTC only demands a four- to five-year commitment after college graduation—at which point officers can choose to quit and do something else. Medicine is, in effect, at least a ten-year commitment: four of medical school, at least three of residency, and at least another three to pay off med school loans. At which point a smiling twenty-two-year-old graduate will be a glum thirty-two-year-old doctor who doesn't entirely get how she got to be a doctor anyway, and might tell her earlier self the things that earlier self didn't know.

Contrast this experience with nursing, which requires only a four-year degree, or PAs, who have two to three years of additional school. As John Goodman points out in "Why Not A Nurse?", nursing is much less heavily or uniformly regulated than doctoring. Nurses can move to Oregon:

SHOULD I GO TO MEDICAL SCHOOL?

Take JoEllen Wynne. When she lived in Oregon, she had her own practice. As a nurse practitioner, she could draw blood, prescribe medication (including narcotics) and even admit patients to the hospital. She operated like a primary care physician and without any supervision from a doctor. But, JoEllen moved to Texas to be closer to family in 2006. She says, "I would have loved to open a practice here, but due to the restrictions, it is difficult to even volunteer." She now works as an advocate at the American Academy of Nurse Practitioners.

And, based on the article, avoid Texas. Over time, we'll see more articles like "Why Nurses Need More Authority: Allowing nurses to act as primary-care providers will increase coverage and lower health-care costs. So why is there so much opposition from physicians?" Doctors will oppose this, because it's in their economic self-interest to avoid more competition.

The next problem with becoming a doctor involves what economists call "information asymmetry." Most undergraduates making life choices don't realize the economic problems I've described above, let alone some of the other problems I'm going to describe here. When I lay out the facts about becoming a doctor to my freshman writing students, many of those who want to be doctors look at me suspiciously, like I'm offering them a miracle weight-loss drug or have grown horns and a tail.

"No," I can see them thinking, "this can't be true because it contradicts so much of what I've been implicitly told by society." They don't *want* to believe. Which is great—right up to the point they have to live their lives, and see how those are lives are being shaped by forces that no one told them about. Just like no one told them about opportunity costs or what residencies are really like.

SHOULD I GO TO MEDICAL SCHOOL?

Medical students and doctors have complained to me about how *no one told them how bad it is*. No one *really* told them, that is. I'm not sure how much of this I should believe, but, at the very least, if you're reading this essay you've been told. I suspect a lot of now-doctors were told or had an inkling of what it's really like, but they failed to imagine the nasty reality of 24- or 30-hour call.

They, like most people, ignore information that conflicts with their current belief system about the glamour of medicine to avoid cognitive dissonance (as we all do: this is part of what Jonathan Haidt points out in *The Righteous Mind*, as does Daniel Kahneman in *Thinking, Fast and Slow*). Many now-doctors, even if they were aware, probably ignored that awareness and now complain—in other words, even if they had better information, they'd have ignored it and continued on their current path. They pay attention to status and money instead of happiness.

For example, Penelope Trunk cites Daniel Gilbert's *Stumbling on Happiness* and says:

Unfortunately, people are not good at picking a job that will make them happy. Gilbert found that people are ill-equipped to imagine what their life would be like in a given job, and the advice they get from other people is bad, typified by some version of "You should do what I did."

Let's examine some other vital takeaways from *Stumbling on Happiness*: [3]

* Making more than about $40,000/year does little to improve happiness (this should probably be greater in, say, NYC, but the main point stands: people think money and happiness show a linear correlation when they really don't).

SHOULD I GO TO MEDICAL SCHOOL?

* Most people value friends, family, and social connections more than additional money, at least once their income reaches about $40K/year. If you're trading time with friends and family for money, or, <u>worse, for commuting</u>, you're making a tremendous, doctor-like mistake.

* Your sex life probably matters more than your job, and many people mis-optimize in this area. I've heard many residents and med students say they're too busy to develop relationships or have sex with their significant others, if they manage to retain one, and this probably makes them really miserable.

* Making your work meaningful is important.

Attend med school without reading Gilbert at your own peril. No one in high school or college warns you of the dangers of seeking jobs that harm your sex life, because high schools are too busy trying to convince you **not** to have a sex life. So I'm going issue the warning: if you take a job that makes you too tired to have sex or too tired to engage in contemporary mate-seeking behaviors, you're probably making a mistake.

The sex-life issue might be overblown, because people who really want to have one find a way to have one. Some med students and residents are just offering the kinds of generic romantic complaints that everyone stupidly offers, and which mean nothing more than discussion about the weather. You can tell what a person really wants by observing what they do, rather than what they say.

But med students and residents have shown enough agony over trade-offs and time costs to make me believe that med school does generate a genuine pall over romantic lives.

SHOULD I GO TO MEDICAL SCHOOL?

There is a correlation-is-not-causation problem—maybe med school attracts the romantically inept—but I'm willing to assume for now that it doesn't.

The title of Trunk's post is "How much money do you need to be happy? Hint: Your sex life matters more." If you're in an industry that consistently makes you too tired for sex, you're doing things wrong and need to re-prioritize. Nurses can work three twelves a week, or thirty-six total hours, and be okay. But, as described above, being a doctor doesn't let employees re-prioritize.

Proto-doctors screw up their 20s and 30s, sexually speaking, because they've committed to a job that's so cruel to its occupants that, if doctors were equally cruel to patients, those doctors would be sued for malpractice. And the student loans mean that med students effectively can't quit. They've traded sex for money and gotten a raw deal. They'll be surrounded by people who are miserable and uptight—and who have also mis-prioritized.

You probably also don't realize how ill-equipped you are to what your life would be like as a doctor because a lot of doctors sugarcoat their jobs, or because you don't know any actual doctors. So you extrapolate from people who say, "That's great" when you say you want to be a doctor. If you say you're going to stay upwind and see what happens, they don't say, "That's great," because they simply think you're another flaky college student. But saying "I want to go to med school" or "I want to go to law school" isn't a good way to seem level-headed (though I took the latter route; fortunately, I had the foresight to quit). Those routes, if they once led to relative success and happiness, don't any more, at least for most people, who can't imagine what life is like on

SHOULD I GO TO MEDICAL SCHOOL?

the other end of the process. With law, at least the process is three years, not seven or more.

No one tells you this because there's still a social and cultural meme about how smart doctors are. Some are. Lots more are very good memorizers and otherwise a bit dull. And you know what? That's okay. Average doctors seeing average patients for average complaints are fixing routine problems. They're directing traffic when it comes to problems they can't solve. Medicine doesn't select for being well-rounded, innovative, or interesting; if anything, it selects *against* those traits through its relentless focus on test scores, which don't appear to correlate strongly with being interesting or intellectual.

Doctors aren't necessarily associating with the great minds of your generation by going to medical school. Doctors may not even really be associating with great minds. They might just be associating with excellent memorizers. I didn't realize this until I met lots of of doctors, had repeated stabs at real conversations with them, and eventually realized that many aren't intellectually curious and imaginative. There are, of course, plenty of smart, intellectually curious doctors, but given the meme about the intelligence of doctors, there are fewer than imagined and plenty who see themselves as skilled technicians and little more.

A lot of doctors are the smartest stupid people you've met. Smart, because they've survived the academic grind. Stupid, because they signed up for med school, which is effectively signing away extraordinarily valuable options. Life isn't a videogame. There is no reset button, no do-over. Once your 20s are gone, they're gone forever.

SHOULD I GO TO MEDICAL SCHOOL?

Maybe your 20s are *supposed* to be confusing. Although I'm still in that decade, I'm inclined to believe this idea. Medical school offers a trade-off: your professional life isn't confusing and you have a clear path to a job and paycheck. If you take that path, your main job is to jump through hoops. But the path and the hoops offer clarity of professional purpose at great cost in terms of hours worked, debt assumed, and, perhaps worst of all, flexibility. Many doctors would be better off with the standard confusion, but those doctors take the clear, well-lit path out of fear—which is the same thing that drives so many bright but unfocused liberal grads into law schools.

I've already mentioned prestige and money as two big reasons people go to med school. Here's another: fear of the unknown. Bright students start med school because it's a clearly defined, well-lit path. Such paths are becoming increasingly crowded. Uncertainty is scary. You can fight the crowd, or you can find another way. Most people are scared of the other way. They shouldn't be, and they wouldn't be if they knew what graduate school paths are like.

For yet another perspective on the issue of not going to med school, see Ali Binazir's "Why you should not go to medical school — a gleefully biased rant," which has more than 500 comments as of this writing. Binazir correctly says there's only one thing that should drive you to med school: "You have only ever envisioned yourself as a doctor and can only derive professional fulfillment in life by taking care of sick people."

If you can only derive professional fulfillment in life by taking care of sick people, however, you should remember that you can do so by being a nurse or a physicians assistant. And

SHOULD I GO TO MEDICAL SCHOOL?

notice the words Binazir chooses: he *doesn't* say, "help people"—he says "taking care of sick people." The path from this feeling to actually taking care of sick people is a long, miserable one. And you should work hard at envisioning yourself as something else before you sign up for med school.

You can help people in all kinds of ways; the most obvious ones are by having specialized, very unusual skills that lots of people value. Alternately, think of a scientist like Norman Borlaug (I only know about him through Tyler Cowen's book *The Great Stagnation*; in it, Cowen also observes that "When it comes to motivating human beings, status often matters at least as much as money." I suspect that a lot of people going to medical school are really doing it for the status).

Bourlag saved millions of lives through developing hardier seeds and through other work as an agronomist. I don't want to say something overwrought and possibly wrong like, "Bourlag has done more to help people than the vast majority of doctors," since that raises all kinds of questions about what "more" and "help" and "vast majority" mean, but it's fair to use him as an example of how to help people outside of being a doctor. Programmers, too, write software that can be instantly disseminated to billions of people, and yet those who want to "help" seldom think of it as a helping profession, even though it is.

For a lot of the people who say they want to be a doctor so they can help people, greater intellectual honesty would lead them to acknowledge mixed motives in which helping people is only one and perhaps not the most powerful. On the other hand, if you really want to spend your professional life taking care of sick people, Binazir is right. But I'm not sure you can really know that before making the decision to go to medical school, and, worse, even if all you want to do is take care of sick people, you're going to find a system stacked against you in that respect.

You're not taking the best care of people at 3 a.m. on a 12- to 24-hour shift in which your supervisors have been screaming at you and your program has been jerking your schedule around like a marionette all month, leaving your sleep schedule out of whack. Yeah, someone has to do it, but it doesn't have to be you, and if fewer people were struggling to become doctors, the system itself would have to change to entice more people into medical school.

One other, minor point: you should get an MD and maybe a PhD if you really, really want to do medical research. But that's a really hard thing for an 18-22 year old to know, and most doctors aren't researchers. Nonetheless, nurses (usually) aren't involved in the same kind of research as research MDs. I don't think this point changes the main thrust of my argument. Superstar researchers are tremendously valuable. If you think you've got the tenacity and curiosity and skills to be a superstar researcher, this essay doesn't apply to you.

Very few people will tell you this, or tell even if you ask; Paul Graham even writes about a doctor friend in his essay "How to do What You Love:"

A friend of mine who is a quite successful doctor complains constantly about her job. When people applying to medical school ask her for advice, she wants to shake them and yell "Don't do it!" (But she never does.) How did she get into this fix? In high school she already wanted to be a doctor. And she is so ambitious and determined that she overcame every obstacle along the way—including, unfortunately, not liking it.

SHOULD I GO TO MEDICAL SCHOOL?

Now she has a life chosen for her by a high-school kid.

When you're young, you're given the impression that you'll get enough information to make each choice before you need to make it. But this is certainly not so with work. When you're deciding what to do, you have to operate on ridiculously incomplete information. Even in college you get little idea what various types of work are like. At best you may have a couple internships, but not all jobs offer internships, and those that do don't teach you much more about the work than being a batboy teaches you about playing baseball.

Having a life chosen for you by a 19-year-old college student or 23-year-old wondering what to do is only marginally better.

I'm not the first person to notice that people don't always understand what they'll be like when they're older; in "Aged Wisdom," Robin Hanson says:

You might look inside yourself and think you know yourself, but over many decades you can change in ways you won't see ahead of time. Don't assume you know who you will become. This applies all the more to folks around you. You may know who they are now, but not who they will become.

This doesn't surprise me anymore. Now I acknowledge that I'm very unlikely to be able to gauge what I'll want in the future.

Contemplate too the psychological makeup of many med students. They're good rule-followers and test-takers; they tend to be very good on tracks but perhaps not so good outside of tracks. Prestige is very important, as is listening to one's elders (who may or may not understand the ways the world is changing in fundamental ways). They may find the real world large and scary, while the academic world is small, highly directed, and sufficiently confined to prevent intellectual or monetary agoraphobia.

These issues are addressed well in two books: *Excellent Sheep* by William Deresiewicz and *Zero to One* by Peter Thiel and Blake Masters. I won't endorse everything in either book, but pay special attention to their discussions of the psychology of elite students and especially the weaknesses that tend to appear in that psychology.

It is not easy for anyone to accept criticism, but that may be particularly true of potential med students, who have been endlessly told how "smart" they are, or supposedly are. Being smart in the sense of passing classes and acing tests may not necessarily lead you towards the right life, and, moreover, graduate schools and consulting have evolved to prey on your need for accomplishment, positive feedback, and clear metrics. You are the food they need to swallow and digest. Think long and hard about that.

If you don't want to read *Excellent Sheep* and *Zero to One*, or think you're "too busy," I'm going to marvel: you're willing to spend hundreds of thousands of dollars and years of your life to a field that you're not wiling to spend $30 and half a day to understanding better? That's a dangerous yet astonishingly common level of willful ignorance.

Another friend asked what I wanted to accomplish with this essay. The small answer: help people understand things they didn't understand before. The larger answer—something like "change medical education"—isn't very plausible because the forces encouraging people to be doctors are so much larger than me. The power of delusion and prestige is so vast that I doubt I can make a difference through writing alone. Almost no writer can: **the best one can hope for is changes at the margin over time**.

Some med school stakeholders are starting to recognize the issues discussed in this essay: for example, *The New York Times* has reported that New York University's med school may be able to shorten its duration from four years to three, and "Administrators at N.Y.U. say they can make the change without compromising quality, by eliminating redundancies in their science curriculum, getting students into clinical training more quickly and adding some extra class time in the summer." This may be a short-lived effort. But it may also be an indicator that word about the perils of med school is spreading.

I don't expect this essay to have much impact. It would require people to a) find it, which most probably won't do, b) read it, which most probably won't do, c) understand it, which most of those who read it won't or can't do, and d) implement it. Most people don't seem to give their own futures much real consideration. I know a staggering number of people who go to law or med or b-school because it "seems like a good idea." Never mind the problem with following obvious paths, or the question of opportunity costs, or the difficulty in knowing what life is like on the other side.

People just don't think that far ahead. I'm already imagining people on the Internet who are thinking about going to med school and who see the length of this essay and decide it's not worth it—as if they'd rather spend a decade of their lives gathering the knowledge they could read in an hour. They just don't understand the low quality of life medicine entails for many if not most doctors.

Despite the above, I will make one positive point about med school: if you go, if you jump through all the hoops, if you make it to the other side, you will have a remunerative job for life, as long as you don't do anything grossly awful. Job demand and pay are important. Law school doesn't offer either anymore. Many forms of academic grad schools are cruel pyramid schemes propagated by professors and universities. But medicine does in fact have a robust job market on the far end. That is a real consideration. You're still probably better off being a nurse or PA—nurses are so in-demand that nursing schools can't grow fast enough, at least as of 2015—but I don't want to pretend that the job security of being a doctor doesn't exist.

I'm not telling you what to do. I rarely tell anyone what to do. I'm describing trade-offs and asking if you understand them. It appears that few people do. Have you read this essay carefully? If not, read it again. Then at least you won't be one of the many doctors who hate what you do, warn others about how doctors are sick of their profession, and wish you'd been wise enough to take a different course.

Footnotes:

[0] Here's another anti-doctor article: "Why I Gave Up Practicing Medicine." Scott Alexander's "Medicine As Not Seen On TV" is also good. The anti-med-school lit is available to those who seek it. Most potential med students don't seem to. Read the literature and understand the perils. If after learning you still want to go anyway, great.

SHOULD I GO TO MEDICAL SCHOOL?

Commenter ktswan went from nursing to med school and writes, "I am much happier in medicine than lots of my colleagues, I think in many ways because I knew exactly what I was getting into, what I was sacrificing, and what I wanted to gain from it."

[1] One could argue that many of the problems in American K-12 education stem from a captive audience whose presence or absence in a school is based on geography and geographical accidents rather than the school's merit.

[2] You can read more about the match lawsuit here. Europe doesn't have a match-like system; there, the equivalent of medical residency is much more like a job.

[3] *Stumbling on Happiness* did more to change my life and perspective than almost any other book. I've read thousands of books. Maybe tens of thousands. Yet this one influences my day-to-day decisions and practices by clarifying how a lot of what people say they value they don't, and how a lot of us make poor life choices based on perceived status that end up screwing us. Which is another way of saying we end up screwing ourselves. Which is what a lot of medical students, doctors, and residents have done. No one holds the proverbial gun to your head and orders you into med school (unless you have exceptionally fanatical parents). When you're *doing* life, at least in industrialized Western countries, you mostly have yourself to blame for your poor choices, made without enough knowledge to know the right choices.

Ed: Many thanks to Jake Seliger of The Story's Story *for granting permission to include his essay.*

SHOULD I GO TO MEDICAL SCHOOL?

Ryan the Naturopath

Toward the end of my second year of med school, I came to many of the same realizations that you have in your post. Okay, to be honest, I realized them before I started, but I had the illusion that once I got in, I could change the system for the better from within. Fat chance of that!

What I realized after those 2 years was that no only was there considerable inertia against any positive change in the system, the momentum behind so many of the negative realities that you and everyone else has detailed is far too great. The system as it stands currently can't last. Fundamental changes are needed, but from where can they come when to change the system would destroy so many of the vested interests of that system?

So, I started looking for another way, and I found it in naturopathy. It's a school of medicine that is focused on guiding patients toward optimum health, not simply the absence of disease. Health is defined as "freedom from limitations." We are only as healthy as the environment in which we live: physical, mental, emotional, and spiritual. It is our job as physicians to assist individuals in removing the limitations from their health. We are health coaches, mentors, and guides on each person's journey to optimizing health.

The naturopathic practice of medicine is based on six key principles:

1. Promote the healing power of nature.
2. First, do no harm. We choose therapies with the intent to keep harmful side effects to a minimum and not to suppress symptoms.

3. Treat the whole person. We recognize that a person's health is affected by many different types of factors, including physical, mental, emotional, genetic, environmental, and social; and we consider all of these factors when choosing therapies and tailor treatment to each patient.
4. Treat the cause. We always seek to identify and treat the causes of a disease or condition, rather than its symptoms. We believe that symptoms are signs that the body is trying to fight disease, adapt to it, or recover from it.
5. Prevention is the best cure. We teach ways of living that have been shown to be most healthy and most likely to prevent illness.
6. The physician is a teacher. We consider it important to educate our patients in taking responsibility for their own health.

Just as important as having all of these principles though (which I'm sure most of you share), we believe in the importance of getting the education and taking the time with patients that's needed to adhere to them. In the realm of education, there are currently 7 accredited naturopathic medical programs in North America, with a new campus opening up next fall in San Diego. For more information, I would encourage you to check out the Association of Accredited Naturopathic Medical Colleges at aanmc.org and keep the faith! Change is coming, and it is possible to be the kind of physician that you'd always imagined that you could be. I'm living proof!

SHOULD I GO TO MEDICAL SCHOOL?

Physical therapy and pharmacology

Most all docs I've worked with have said they wouldn't do it again or recommend it to their kids. Despite that, I do remember 3 or 4 who truly loved what they did. I suspect they knew this before entering medical school and did not apply for prestige, income, authority, respect, etc. So yes, those people are out there.

However, the sacrifices all of them make are very real and reflected in the original article and my post above, albeit in a harsh and bitter tone. I'd suggest looking up alcohol/drug abuse, divorce and suicide rates among physicians compared to other professions simply to point out comparative stress levels. An OB/GYN relative of mine had two attempts herself.

As for myself since the post above, I've moved on to an ancillary health profession similar to posters above doing PT and Pharm. I have a 40-hr week, a very nice paycheck, no malpractice, no insurance hassle, lots of time with the wife and kids, ability to relocate almost anywhere, in very high demand, and I still help people. I've set up a life for myself that I couldn't have begun to have in medicine, nor can my engineer brother or attorney sister-in-law. For me it is a much improved lifestyle and I wouldn't go back for anything.

I'm glad there are those few who truly enjoy it because it's certainly a noble and needed profession. I just feel sad for those who are unhappy doing it but are stuck from debt, mortgage, kids, as well as those who simply do it for their own ego. In older times it was respected. Today nobody cares that you're a doc except family members and other docs.

SHOULD I GO TO MEDICAL SCHOOL?

Clearly different people are fulfilled by different means and some will love medicine for its challenge, responsibility, and impact on patients lives. So for anyone reading this, maybe medicine is your place and you know you'll love it. However, even then the sacrifices are still very real, so do your research, shadow several docs and ask the hard uncomfortable questions before applying.

For anyone else applying because parents expect it (as was my case) or income, ego, status or whatever other reason I highly recommend against it and predict deep disappointment. There are other options that provide more personal time, money, status or whatever else it is you're looking for that don't put the lives of patients at risk while you figure it out. That's one other reason I left. I knew that my discontented attitude was inherently leading to a disservice to my patients despite really wanting to do my best for them. My heart simply wasn't in it. Good luck.

SHOULD I GO TO MEDICAL SCHOOL?

The pharmacist lifestyle

My hubby is a pharmacist – working 50-60 hours per week and is earning close to $200,000. No liability (his insurance is $200 per year), and he comes home to no worries. He deals with Assisted Living so no contact with patients which is nice. He has 3-4 weeks vacation, plus all holidays, and paternity leave of 3 months off. Most family docs, internists, pediatricians etc. make less than that and have to go through a much harder life. Our quality of life is great! Always vacationing or with family and friends.

SHOULD I GO TO MEDICAL SCHOOL?

The unemployed pharmacist

I recently graduated from pharmacy school that was a 6 year program out of high school. I wanted to do medicine when I entered college but had doubts from what I was hearing. I did *not* want to do medicine for the money, but rather because I absolutely love anatomy, physiology and biological sciences and love the idea of lifelong learning.

Anyway, I was doubtful I'd get into medical school from the start, so I went with pharmacy school. The material was dry, but my family was convinced it would be good for me as it would be less stressful, with a good pay and stability. I didn't enjoy learning about drugs and therapeutics, but stayed in pharmacy school because of the pathophysiology believing clinical pharmacy might be an option for me.

In 2010, pharmacy started to undergo a major saturation due to an increased number of schools, leading to an increased number of graduates that exceeded the number of pharmacist jobs available. At that time, I was in my first year trying to find a pharmacy internship. A majority of pharmacy students work at internships during school — in retail, hospital, and occasionally long-term care — to gain experience during school. Before, getting an internship was more a preparation for real-world work, but now it is an *absolute must* if you want to work.

I tried every retail, hospital, and independent pharmacy I could. I sent my résumé everywhere. I asked my parents to forward my resume to people they knew. Nobody came up with anything. I struggled for 3 years trying to find a student internship and graduated empty-handed.

SHOULD I GO TO MEDICAL SCHOOL?

So I found out the reality of working in pharmacy when I did my student rotations. One of my *best* rotations was my internal medicine one. I worked alongside doctors, rounding in the ward, attending morning and noon conferences. I was enjoying this so much, while the other pharmacy intern with me absolutely hated the extra learning that the medical doctors were required to do. I learned so much more in a week than I did in my 5 years of schooling and was so eager to consider a career in medicine again.

However, remaining realistic, I graduated and decided to work a little before jumping the gun. The issue is that without intern experience, I wasn't able to get a post-graduate residency nor a job at all. In hospital, it is getting near impossible to get a job without a residency; now imagine trying without any intern experience at all. Retail is tough but doable if I move to a rural/remote location. For medical and personal reasons, I can't do that at this time.

So I'm 4 months out of school and unemployed. I applied to 30+ hospitals with no word and am incredibly frustrated. I'm looking into government positions or health startup companies that have openings for clinical positions. This is definitely a tough job search and I am still romanticizing the thought of medical school for the near future.

However, I also have generalized anxiety that I fear would make medical school an unrealistic choice for me, no matter how exciting it sounds right now. I appreciate your honesty and definitely have had these sentiments from many in the medical profession. Many people who I know are doctors are indifferent or unhappy with the way medicine is going, but some of the articles above seem that some people still love what they do.

SHOULD I GO TO MEDICAL SCHOOL?

I never had an avid social life; barely made any close friends in school, so that's not really a concern. However, I do burn out and get stressed and anxious more easily than I'd like to admit. I hope I find a job first and figure out eventually if med school is for me. I'm 23 now and would probably be looking at 27-28 to enter med school.

SHOULD I GO TO MEDICAL SCHOOL?

A little time for microbiology

I just want to thank you from the depths of my being and the bottom of my heart for this post! As a returning adult student (not old at 26, but returning) at The University of Texas at Austin and a former pre-med student, I am in classes with a lot of seniors going to medical school next year and who are starting to do their interviews.

While part of me feels a jealous longing to be doing the same, I also have a passion for teaching and education, and have decided the right path for me is to become a professor of Microbiology, rather than a doctor. It was therapeutic to realize that my choice seems right, that the pressures and nightmares accompanying med school and the medical profession are as real as I had heard from indirect sources. I'll stop wishing I were interviewing for med schools now, and start feeling sorry for my classmates that are!

Ed: It is also possible to find your calling and do your thing without putting other people down.

SHOULD I GO TO MEDICAL SCHOOL?

Research career

I finished the MD and went into research. Most of my days are 9 to 5, but I love the lab, I don't have to deal with enormous amounts of people like patients, bosses, other arrogant doctors — so many big egos! And I have hobbies! I make little money, but I have no debt as of now.

My wife is a doc, and she does it because she can only see herself caring for patients. She did it for the right reason. I did it to feel important and it was stupid; thank god I found research. Pays little, but I bike to the rock climbing site.

SHOULD I GO TO MEDICAL SCHOOL?

The happy Nurse Practitioner

I'm a NP that is thinking about going to Med School. Oh, let me change that. I'm a NP that *was* thinking about going to med school. I'm making $85,0000 per year. I work for a hospice company part-time seeing patients in their homes making $125 per visit. I'm staying right where I am.

SHOULD I GO TO MEDICAL SCHOOL?

Dr Angove, Doctor of Osteopathic Medicine

As an almost octogenarian retired general surgeon I can enjoy all the essays above.

When I was fourteen I was inspired to be a medical missionary. At Westmar College, my counsellor directed me to take courses that would credential me as a biology, chemistry and physics high school teacher; a pastor; and physician.

I started teaching with an annual salary of $3500. After three very enjoyable years of renovating the third floor of the high school with all the most up-to-date scientific equipment through a grant from the U.S. government who wanted us to catch up to the developers of Sputnik, I studied physics at the University of Iowa with Dr. Wernher von Braun who invented the rockets that bombarded London, and Dr. Van Allen after whom the radiation belt circling the earth was named, and watched the development of the Explorer.

I was going to become an M.D., but after my wife experienced a disablingly painful back condition that couldn't be helped at the hospital in Iowa City, she wanted to see her own physician in Rochester, MN who after fifteen minutes had her laughing as she walked normally out of his office, and at no charge to her. After learning that he was a D.O., I questioned many M.D.s as to what is a D.O. As with some of the above comments I received very discouraging advice; but my real life experience told me to get my D.O. degree for which I am eternally grateful.

This past weekend a beautiful princess and a shy gentle boy invited me to celebrate their fiftieth wedding anniversary.

SHOULD I GO TO MEDICAL SCHOOL?

Their pediatrician daughter from Florida asked me to attend the celebration of which I was their pastor for three years in Madrid, Iowa, and performed the marriage ceremony. We had two daughters while teaching, another daughter while studying osteopathic medicine in Des Moines, Iowa, where I am now a board of trustees member of the great Des Moines University. Two sons while in Surgical residency; and another daughter during my first year of surgical practice in Milwaukee, WI.

My malpractice insurance policy was $1000/yr. Then suddenly $16,000/yr and at that time many surgeons questioned whether to continue doing surgery; well the last year of practice I went to the bank to borrow $104,000. to buy the policy required to practice surgery in the hospital. My first surgery in Milwaukee was an appendectomy for which I charged $170. The parents insisted on paying me in cash; and greeted me by bowing and saying: Good morning Mr. Doctor. I don't even know what the charge for an appendectomy is now.

A few years ago I did a cholecystectomy on Governor Adelberto Paz in La Clinica Medica Cristiana in Progeso, Yoro, Honduras for $75 charged by the hospital. I didn't charge anything. My kids have often asked: Dad, why do we always go on vacation to some place where you do surgery? It's because that's what I enjoy doing the most! My oldest daughter Julie is a labor and delivery nurse and stops in to tell me excitedly: "Dad, I had the most wonderful day… and they even paid me for it!"

I've been mentoring premed students from the University of Wisconsin and Marquette University and having them with me at the Surgical Morbidity/Mortality Reviews, and all have thanked me for inspiring them. A beautiful girl who could be a model came up to me at the Medical Society Foundation dinner and told me: Thank you Dr. Angove for inspiring me to become a general surgeon. That's worth more than any amount of money. My advice to young people is to put all your resources into becoming that which is your passion and what God inspires your heart and mind to be to serve humanity. A cheerful heart is like a good medicine!

SHOULD I GO TO MEDICAL SCHOOL?

Veterinary medicine

So many of these are true now for veterinary medicine as well. Add on to your list that clients expect top-notch cutting-edge veterinary medical care that is essentially free (e.g. "Can't you just give it a shot?" or "Vet bills are so expensive" even when they are a very tiny fraction of what human medicine would charge) and then maintain that you're "not a real doctor." Despite paying about the same (I think vet med recently became more expensive), you get a much lower salary. Speaking of the dangers of medicine, how frequently do your patients scratch, bite, kick, or maul one of your colleagues?
It's all getting out of hand, and I don't recommend vet school to people either, unless they come from a very wealthy background and can pay for it upfront.

SHOULD I GO TO MEDICAL SCHOOL?

Biomedical Engineering & Master's of Public Health

I was a medical school applicant back in 2000. I actually was on the waiting list and missed admission by about 8 spots in 2001. I could have reapplied but changed my mind. I decided to continue with my career in biomedical engineering. I earned an MS in Bioengineering back in the late 90s.

Years later, I was working on electronic health records for a government job. I decided to earn a 2nd Master's of Public Health. I wanted to go deeper in the details of the healthcare system. I embarked on a new round of research and a rigorous curriculum. We studied the extreme details of the history of Medicare, Medicaid, health economics, policy analysis, eligibility determination, medical billing, healthcare finance, epidemiology, etc. I did a capstone project on Agent Orange and its impact on the VA healthcare system.

In 2008 we had to compare and contrast the healthcare proposals by each presidential candidate. It was very interesting, and we knew healthcare reform was pending. I learned a huge amount about the system.

My conclusion is that the healthcare system does need major reform. The focus should most definitely be on primary care such as family practice, pediatrics, internal medicine, etc. But the flawed Medicare payment system based on fee-for-service created a ridiculous problem spanning decades. The system tends to favor specialists like radiologists (as you noted). But that is economically inefficient. The focus should be on primary care like in France which has the #1 system ranked by the World Health Organization.

SHOULD I GO TO MEDICAL SCHOOL?

The US spends the most on healthcare but gets the least return on investment compared to other countries. There is an extreme shortage of primary care. They are woefully underpaid and overworked. You are 100% right. A person should choose an MD only if the desire is to care for patients.

The high-paying specialties like dermatology and radiology need to be scaled back. The focus needs to switch to primary care. The MD/PhD also needs to be scaled back. But primary care is blatantly overwhelmed and discriminated against (in my opinion).

Meanwhile, I am glad I continued to stay in biomedical engineering. I am working on a 3rd master's in ME and hope to do a PhD. I would like to focus on 3-D printing and OpenGL programming with applications to medical device manufacturing. I also saw veterans with prosthetic legs in a race in Texas. I am also interested in prosthetic devices and mechanical design with Solidworks or finite element analysis and continuum mechanics.

I'm really glad I chose to stay in biomedical engineering rather than go to medical school. I recommend alternatives to medical school like a graduate degree in health informatics, FDA regulatory affairs, biomedical engineering, MBA in healthcare finance, accounting and medical billing electives, etc. The demand is very high and pay is good.

SHOULD I GO TO MEDICAL SCHOOL?

PA vs NP vs MD

Someone else commented, "I realized how soul-sucking, petty, isolating, unrewarding, and alienating the culture of research was, and decided to leave research." Ha! You have no idea how much worse it is in medicine. Soul-sucking, petty, isolating, alienating, all of it.

Seeing how patients are treated according to their insurance policy is soul sucking. Listening to the attending and residents laugh about a patient who just coded and died is soul sucking. Petty doesn't even *begin* to describe the childish, egotistical, passive-aggressive behavior you will be subjected to day in and day out. Isolation and alienation is par for the course.

You will spend your days in the library and in the bowels of the hospital. You will drive home, completely drained and exhausted, and look at people out playing volleyball, or having a barbecue in the park, and you will envy them for having a normal life.

If you are single, as I am, you will come home to an empty, dirty apartment you have no time to clean and try to distract yourself from how lonely you are. You will stop answering your phone because it is just too miserable to keep saying "no" to your friends. Eventually they stop calling. You will be broke, living off loans. Every time you buy something you will feel a twinge of guilt and try not to think about how much it will cost with interest.

I will be graduating from PA school mid-August, so perhaps I can give you some-on-the-ground perspective to help you with your decision on NP vs PA vs MD. I have many years of experience working in the medical field as a CNA at a nursing home & hospice, a medical assistant at a free clinic for the uninsured, as well as a pharmacy tech. I agree 100% with Dr Binazir that if you do not enjoy taking care of sick people, you are setting yourself up for misery, especially as a mid-level practitioner. Doctors can always escape to specialties where they have minimal contact with patients, but as a mid-level you will be a bedside provider, doing a great deal of grunt work working directly with miserable, sick people every day.

Vanderbilt's accelerated NP program sounds a bit iffy to me. Though I don't know a whole lot about it, I can say that all the NPs I know have had years of experience as a nurse before going to NP school, and that the advanced nursing degree was traditionally meant to add to that experience. Going through nursing school to emerge as an NP may be a disadvantage to your career. Secondly, NPs are trained to practice advanced nursing, not medicine. The coursework is typically thin on the hard sciences. As for the perceived autonomy available to NPs vs. PAs, that is really a terrible reason to pursue an advanced nursing degree. Virtually all NPs in practice work under the direction of a physician and will be the first to tell you that practicing independently would be dangerous.

PA school is like accelerated med school. You take most of the pre-clinical science such as pharmacology, cadaver anatomy, and pathophysiology, in addition to clinical medicine, which is taught by organ system. There is a very strong emphasis on learning how to do a thorough physical exam and history. This is the one area I believe that PAs often excel at in comparison to MD/DOs. That is by design.

SHOULD I GO TO MEDICAL SCHOOL?

As a PA, you won't be expected to diagnose and manage complex patients on your own, but the docs you work for *must* be able to trust your exam and documentation skills. Due to the accelerated nature of PA curriculum, however, there is quite a bit that is glossed over. You aren't expected to understand the deep pathophysiology of the diseases you study. It is more clinical nuts and bolts, as some have called it, "cookbook medicine." To get an idea of what you would be missing, just flip through a USMLE review book vs a PANCE review book.

That being said, do not make the mistake of thinking PA school is easier than med school. Yes, it is significantly shorter, but there is simply so much thrown at you in such a short period of time, it is overwhelming and there is very little hand-holding. There are no summer breaks. It's an unrelenting grind.

Also, PA schools usually have very strict remediation policies. Where I went, if you scored below an 80% on any exam, you were given one chance to remediate. If you scored below 80% on remediation, you were kicked out of school, sink or swim, no exceptions. This happened to a few of my friends, and the overall washout rate at my school was typically between 15%-25%. The stress of losing your entire career and being dismissed from school tens of thousands in debt over one exam is at times unbearable. It was not uncommon for some girl to start sobbing after an exam, which is quite unnerving. There were girls in my class whose hair was falling out.

SHOULD I GO TO MEDICAL SCHOOL?

Final thoughts

After medical school, after trying my hand at startups management consulting, I started a writing and publishing business. I wrote my first book, The Tao of Dating: The Thinking Man's Enlightened Guide to Success with Women in 2005, and my second one, *The Tao of Dating: The Smart Woman's Guide to Being Absolutely Irresistible* in 2009.

I've given many seminars and talks, and have received over 5000 letters from people regarding their love lives. And I can tell you this: there's a lot of similarity between dating and choosing a career.

There's "Bright Shiny Object" syndrome: she's got great hair and a kickin' bod, so you go for it — only to have a disastrous breakup or divorce down the road, because you had conveniently decided to overlook her alcoholism.

There's "Hey This Is What I Should Be Doing, Right?" syndrome: you're just kind of dating someone, then you're just kind of engaged, then you're just kind of married with 2.3 kids, and how the hell did I get here?

There's "Tall, Dark, Handsome and Rich" syndrome. He looked perfect on paper! So you married him, even though you two were fundamentally incompatible and he was kind of a jerk.

My point: big-ticket decisions like career choice and partner selection are remarkably similar. And it's very easy for people to get distracted by their cognitive biases and heuristics, only

SHOULD I GO TO MEDICAL SCHOOL?

to make a disastrous decision they come to regret years later when it's too late.

When it comes to dating and choosing a career, the most important thing is *fit*: is this a good choice *for you*? Is it a good temperamental match? Does this enhance your sense of meaning and purpose in life? Do you feel yourself flourishing in its context, or stifled? Are the quirks something you're willing to put up with, or deal breakers?

The better you can answer these questions, the better decision you can make regarding your career. And you can answer these questions better by *knowing yourself*. So go forth and know yourself! Take some legitimate online career test (Myers-Briggs and Enneagram are total pseudoscience bullshit, by the way). Go to some legitimate aptitudes testing place, like the Johnson-O'Connor Human Engineering Lab (did that some time ago; not cheap but very thorough). Take up meditation so you get in better touch with your own feelings. Ask your old friends for their opinion; usually, they know you better than you do.

One of the main purposes of this book is to weed out the 98% of med school applicants who are going into it for the wrong reasons. That's why I've said a lot of strongly-worded things in this book about how terrible the medical profession is. But if you've read this far and you still think that yeah, you want to do it, then by all means, go for it. If you are part of the 2% who with clear eyes, zero illusions and a calm heart know that taking care of patients is your calling and your fate, the world needs you. Especially if you're going into primary care, 'cause the world *really* needs you. Go forth and heal, and let me know how it goes:
drali(at)shouldigotomedicalschool.com

SHOULD I GO TO MEDICAL SCHOOL?

8. ADDITIONAL RESOURCES

A Survey of America's Physicians, commissioned by The Physicians Foundation

A September 2012 survey by The Physicians Foundation found that 6 out of 10 physicians would quit today if they could. You can download the full pdf of the report, A Survey of America's Physicians: Practice Patterns and Perspectives.

Works by Atul Gawande, M.D.
To deeply understand what the practice of medicine is like, I recommend the works of Atul Gawande. You can start with his *New Yorker* pieces, and then dig into his books if you want more. Also, before comparing yourself to him, please note that Gawande is kind of superhuman: full-time surgeon, Professor at both Harvard Medical School and the Harvard School of Public Health, winner of a Rhodes and a MacArthur, and staff writer at the *New Yorker*.
The heroism of incremental care from *The New Yorker*
Complications: A Surgeon's Notes on an Imperfect Science
Better: A Surgeon's Notes on Performance
Being Mortal: Medicine and What Matters in the End

SHOULD I GO TO MEDICAL SCHOOL?

Works by Sandeep Jauhar, M.D.
Why Doctors Are Sick of Their Profession from *The Wall Street Journal*
Intern: A Doctor's Initiation
Doctored: The Disillusionment of an American Physician

Why I walked away from a $250,000/year salary
Alida Brandenburg wrote a very candid 4-part series about how she decided to leave medicine:
Part One: And in the Beginning...
Part Two: And in the Thick of It...
Part Three: And in the The End...
Part Four: My Jerry Springer "Final Thought"

NOVA: The Doctor's Diaries
Follow the lives of seven people over two decades, as they move from Harvard Medical School to midlife. Aired April 7, 2009 on PBS.

Pre-meds: the caffeine addicted, cut-throat, control lovers from The Prospect

The Bullying Culture of Medical School, by Pauline W. Chen., M.D.

The MD Burnout Epidemic by Carleen Wild. Is your doctor ailing? A new study suggests he might be.

Do Residencies Make Doctors-in-Training Depressed? by Stav Ziv in Newsweek

SHOULD I GO TO MEDICAL SCHOOL?

Malcolm Gladwell: "Tell People What It's Really Like To Be A Doctor" by Robert Pearl, M.D. in Forbes.com

How Being a Doctor Became the Most Miserable Profession by Daniela Drake in The Daily Beast

Made in the USA
Las Vegas, NV
29 November 2020